W9-BLO-291

Read What Others Are Saying About This Book ...

"After two decades of caregiving for seven elders and writing my own book, plus blogs, a forum, radio shows and a newspaper column, you'd think I'd have it all down.

However, The Elder Care Survival Guide will now be one of my chief references as I continue to help other caregivers survive."

— Carol Bradley Bursack, *Minding Our Elders*

"The Elder Care Survival Guide is my go-to reference, placed in one of the most important positions on my desk — right next to my dictionary and thesaurus."

— Denise M. Brown, Founder, Caregiving.com
Take Comfort and *The Caregiving Years, Six Stages to a Meaningful Journey*

"The Elder Care Survival Guide has just the right amount of heart so that the overwhelmed caregiver feels as if the book was written just for them."

— Sally Jo Button, M.Ed.,M.S., CFP®
Faculty Member, Society of Certified Senior Advisors

"Martin writes with a personal touch that made me feel like he was sitting beside me, answering my questions personally."

— Cindi Dawson
Staunton, Virginia

"Owning a copy of The Elder Care Survival Guide is like having both a good road map and a good friend by your side while you make this sometimes frustrating, often maddening, and occasionally supremely rewarding journey of caring for an aging adult."

— Molly Shomer
Head Coach, The ElderCare Team
Eldercareteam.com

"Reading this book is like having a conversation with a knowledgeable and wise friend ... this is the book I've been waiting for someone to write."

— Connie Goldman
The Gifts of Caregiving — Stories of Hardship, Hope and Healing

"The "Eldercare Survival Guide" may become one of a caregiver's best friends ... The chapters on financial considerations and options reveal Martin's expertise as both an eldercare and financial advisor ... Read it as soon as you become aware of your awesome caregiver responsibilities."

— Alan Stanford
Founder and CEO, My Health Care Manager

"Martin takes readers, caregivers, and family members by the hand and gives them the knowledge, confidence, and power to achieve a better life for themselves and their elderly loved one. A must read for all adult children."

— Carol Marak
Founder, Workingcaregiver.com and Carebuzz.com

"Thank you, thank you, thank you for writing this book.I truly appreciate you for presenting these difficult issues in your calm and reassuring manner that eldercare problems can be resolved with love and respect for all parties involved."

— Mark Hendricks
Trilby, Florida

Martin Sabel walks you hand in hand through the most common and difficult situations you'll face as a caregiver.

His practical, step-by-step instructions and resources give you the knowledge and confidence to face your caregiver challenges in a kind and loving way.

— Roger Carr

The Elder Care Survival Guide

How To Care For Aging Parents Without Losing Your Money, Your Family or Your Mind

ISBN #978-0-9822520-0-0

Cover and Interior Layout by Sheila Fredrickson | www.LookGreatInPrint.com

The Elder Care Survival Guide

How To Care For Aging Parents Without Losing Your Money, Your Family or Your Mind

Martin R. Sabel

Silver Sage Publishing, LLC

Table of Contents

Acknowledgements

No book is ever written without the help of others. This one is no different. This book began about 2 years ago when I realized so many of my clients arrived completely unprepared for one of this generation's greatest emotional, health and financial challenges.

Providing care for an aging family member is life altering. In many ways, so is writing a book.

I specifically want to thank my wife, Kathy, for her immeasurable support as I wrote, researched, re-wrote, researched and re-wrote. Her love and understanding made it possible for me to concentrate on the daily efforts to bring this book to life.

To my son, Spencer, thank you for understanding the time spent writing this book, while it reduced the time we could spend together, it will benefit thousands of families struggling with important family decisions.

My parents, Sidney and Miriam Sabel, are shining examples of self-reliance, determination, community and support. It was my dad's health issues in 1994 that opened my eyes to America's fractured health care system and set me on the road of helping families facing late life health and financial issues.

To Robert Freedman and James Mulder, two of the finest elder law and estate planning attorneys I've ever met, thanks for your integrity, skill, judgment and sense of caring. It's an honor to associate with fine men like the two of you.

I've been blessed with a group of special friends whose encouragement, ideas, intelligence and sense of humor provide me energy and direction. Thanks to Mark Hendricks for his steady support, marketing savvy, focus and friendship. Thanks to David Perdew for his clear-eyed business smarts and willingness to listen. To Cindi Dawson, thanks for getting me off my butt to write this book, your infectious positive outlook on life and your insight. To Sheila Fredrickson, thank you for making this so attractive. Your layout skills are masterful. To Criss Bertling and Marie Kane, I appreciate your honesty, willing input and direction. To Dr. Ron Capps, thanks for your support and the occasional kicks in the pants.

To my fellow professionals and elder care advocates—Tom Day of the National Care Planning Council, Dr. Marion Somers, work/life expert Joy Loverde, Molly Shomer of The Eldercare Team, Carol Bradley Bursack, Denise Brown at Caregiving.com, geriatric communications expert David Solie, Gary Crooms of Senior Information Services of America, Alan Stanford of MyHealthCareManager.com, Mark Crews, R.F.G, CSA of Strategic C.A.R.E Planning, Merle D. Griff, Ph.D. of Sarah Adult Day Care, and Russell Gainer of SeniorBridge, Inc. — the lives of elders and those caring for them are better because of you. You have my admiration and deepest appreciation.

To the thousand of families who have shared their stories with me and trusted me over the years to navigate them safely over some of the twisting, bumpy roads known as elder care, you have inspired and educated me in ways you will never know.

Finally, to you the reader of this book, you would not be holding it in your hands unless you truly wanted the best possible result for an aging family member you truly care about. The role of a caregiver can be arduous. It takes a special person to shoulder that responsibility. Thank you for being the caring person that you are. This book is written for you.

— *Martin R. Sabel*

Special Note To My Readers

I have designed this book to provide accurate and authoritative information regarding caring for an elderly loved one.

It is provided with the understanding I am not engaged in rendering any legal, accounting, or other professional services herein.

While it may contain information and general advice regarding health care, legal matters, accounting, and investments, nothing contained in this report should be considered medical, legal, accounting, or investment advice.

This material is not a substitute for personalized advice from a competent and knowledgeable professional who is licensed to practice within his or her field in your state. For specific advice for your situation, always consult an expert.

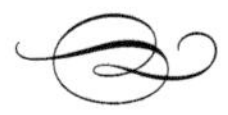

Six Definite Benefits You'll Gain By Reading This Book

Thank you for reading this book.

Chances are you are holding it in your hands because you have an aging parent or other relative who is declining in health. You may be finding yourself in the role of a primary caregiver, or you may worry this will soon be the case.

If you feel scared and overwhelmed by it all, I understand. Caregiving has a lot of moving parts. It can get pretty confusing at times. The problem has two root causes. One stems from America's medical delivery system. It's fragmented and was not intended to address our new longer life spans. The other is our social systems. The phenomenon of a generation simultaneously caring for parents, our self and our children started a bit over 10 years ago. Because it's so new, society is still grappling with the best way to approach it. Our social systems have only recently begun to address the needs you are now facing. They have a long way to go.

That's why I wrote this book: to help you navigate these largely unchartered waters, to make your life easier.

Inside these pages you will discover where to find help, the important questions to ask, the critical information you will need to ensure your loved one remains independent as long as possible, what steps to take first, how to get your siblings to cooperate (and how to respond if they don't), and where to find money for your loved one's care.

This book is meant to be used.

It is loaded with hundreds of proven tips, strategies, and resources that will save you time, money, headaches, and heartaches. As you go through it, make it your own. Dog ear the pages which are important to you. Use a yellow highlighter so key passages will stand out to you. Scribble reminders and insights in the margins.

Use the tips that follow. Over time, you will find yourself growing into a more confident, less stressed caregiver.

The challenge of caregiving may have you feeling isolated and alone right now. Given the state of our medical and social systems right now, I understand why you may feel that way.

The truth is you are not alone.

There is a vast and growing pool of help waiting for you to tap into it. The key is to know it's there and how to find the right people and organizations to help you. You are moving in the right direction because much of that information is right here.

The better you understand the various aspects of caregiving, the better prepared you will be to help your parents as they age. Caring for an aging loved one is one of the toughest "on the job training" experiences you will ever go through. It may get difficult for you at times. You will likely hit a number of bumps in the road along the way. It's all part of the caregiving landscape. The secret is to know these bumps are coming so you will be prepared rather than surprised.

I'll show you how.

Whether you are knee deep in a caregiving crisis, or wondering if it's time for you to get more involved, the answers are waiting for you here.

I want you to do yourself a big favor, too.

Take care of yourself.

There is no law anywhere which says you have to tackle caregiving all alone or that you have to "reinvent the caregiving wheel." I've provided plenty of resources throughout this guide so you won't have to do either of these things.

Please view this book as your personal Elder Care Survival Guide. Put it to use. Then, let me know how it helps you. If you run into a caregiving situation you would like help with, feel free to e-mail me at **martin@SurvivingEldercare.com**

While I can't guarantee I'll come up with a perfect solution, I'm glad to help out as best I can. Thanks, again, for reading this book. Let me know how I can help you.

All my best to you,

— Martin Sabel, "Mr. Eldercare"
Martin@SurvivingEldercare.com

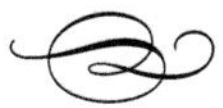

Reader-Only Resources And Updates

Thanks to the Internet, I am able to expand the information available to make your life easier and keep the information in this book up-to-date. Throughout the book I've provided links to more tips, strategies, forms and resources located on a special website set up exclusively for my readers at **http://www.SurvivingEldercare.com.**

It is password protected so only book readers can have access to it. Please go there now to check it out. Registration is free for readers of this book.

As I come across new resources, tips, ideas, and techniques, I'll post them there for you. If you register your copy of the book while you are there, you will also receive free gifts from me from time to time that will make caregiving less expensive and less challenging for you, too.

"It is one of the most beautiful compensations of this life that no man can sincerely try to help another without helping himself."

~ Ralph Waldo Emerson

CHAPTER 1

Do Your Parents Really Need Your Help?

- Warning Signs To Heed
- When To Speak Up; When To Wait
- A Shocking Cause of Health Danger Doctors Don't Discuss

One of the biggest issues you will face will be recognizing when it's time to step in and help your parents. As your parents get older, stay alert for signs that your help is needed. It's easy for them to minimize or cover up their frailty when you only see them for short periods of time. If your parents are married, it is also common for one to cover for the other.

Follow Your Gut Instincts

If you visit and get a funny feeling that something might be amiss, follow those gut instincts and investigate further. Keep alert for any of the following signs. I have indicated some of the possible causes for each symptom. I'm not a doctor, and there can certainly be root causes other than those listed. What is important to understand is that some of what you might see may be simple to solve.

23 Warning Signs Your Parent May Need Help

What You Notice	Possible Causes
Yard is not well maintained; weeds have sprouted; plants are dying	Muscle weakness, balance issues, arthritis pain, cognitive impairment, depression
House is not as well kept as usual	Muscle weakness, balance issues, arthritis pain, cognitive impairment, depression, poor eyesight
Outside light bulbs are burned out	Balance issues, arthritis pain, cognitive impairment, depression
Hallways and rooms are littered with newspapers, signs of hoarding	Cognitive impairment, dementia, depression
Garage is dangerous to walk into	Cognitive impairment, dementia, depression
Low supplies of food, food in the pantry or refrigerator is spoiled or out of date	Muscle weakness, inability to drive, dementia, depression
Burn marks on counter tops, pots, and pans	Forgetfulness, cognitive impairment, depression
Stacks of unopened mail, overdue bills	Poor eyesight, financial difficulties, depression, cognitive impairment
Minimum payments on credit cards	Financial difficulties, memory impairment
Use of walls or furniture to steady themselves while walking	Muscle weakness, poor nutrition, drug interaction, drug or alcohol abuse

Abnormal weight gain	Lack of exercise, drug interactions, depression, thyroid issues
Abnormal weight loss	Mouth pain causing eating discomfort, arthritis pain preventing use of cooking equipment, drug interactions, cognitive impairment, depression, thyroid issues
Less attention to personal hygiene (body odor, hair unwashed/uncombed)	Cognitive impairment
Seeming forgetful	Stress, depression, infection, drug interactions, dementia
Having difficulty moving around	Muscle weakness, arthritis pain, foot sores, coordination difficulties
Difficulty with balance	Muscle weakness, poor nutrition, ear infection, poor eyesight, sore feet, drug interaction, drug or alcohol abuse
Trouble dressing themselves	Muscle weakness, arthritis, poor eyesight, cognitive impairment
Dents and dings on car and/or garage	Poor eyesight, poor distance judgment, coordination problems, impaired physical response, cognitive impairment

This list is by no means complete. Other signs to watch for include incontinence, mental confusion, inability to remember important family information such as birthdays and anniversaries, signs of depression, and not staying socially active.

Consider these warning signs like a weathervane that is pointing to a change in the direction of your mom or dad's health. When you notice a shift in their condition, speak up. If you wait, it could grow into a full-blown crisis.

ELDER FACTS

According to census figures, about 6.5 million older people need assistance with daily living activities. As the number of older Americans continues to increase, this number is expected to double by 2020. Source: Assisted Living Federation of America (ALFA)

For the most part, you will know something is wrong just by using your eyes, ears, nose, and common sense. If you notice changes, don't panic. Talk to other family members. Let them know your concerns so you can begin mapping out a plan.

Four Conditions Requiring Instant Action!

You need to be aware of issues that could quickly become potentially life or health threatening. Any condition that directly impacts your loved one's immediate health and safety requires instant intervention. If you notice any of the following, it is time to act immediately:

- If your mom is not able to physically move
- If your dad wanders out of the house and gets lost
- If there is no food in the house
- If utilities have been turned off

Most times when you visit your parents, you see things that may be risky, but not critical enough to require immediate action. You may have to address the situation in a measured way, but it's not necessary to barge in immediately and start making changes.

> ***ELDER FACTS***
>
> *Most older adults — 4 out of 5 — live with one or more chronic conditions.*

A Shocking Cause of Health Decline Doctors Don't Discuss

Did you notice how many times "drug interactions" were mentioned as possible causes for health issues? It's an area most of us don't think much about, but with seniors it is a very real problem.

So is medication mismanagement.

Improper use of prescription and over-the-counter drugs is a significant and growing issue among seniors. Nearly 50 percent of all adverse medical effects happen to people over the age of 60. Sometimes the problem comes from the medical community. Other times, it's our parents themselves.

ELDER FACTS

Older adults are at increased risk of serious adverse drug events, including falls, depression, confusion, hallucinations and malnutrition, which are an important cause of illness, hospitalization and death among these patients.

It's no secret that as age increases, so do chronic health conditions. Because medicine has become so specialized, it's common for our parents to have a number of doctors:

- a cardiologist for the heart
- an electro-cardiologist for their pacemakers
- a rheumatologist for arthritis
- an allergist for gluten intolerance
- an ophthalmologist for macular degeneration
- an oncologist for cancer, and
- a general practitioner for their general medical needs.

You would like to think the primary care physician acts in the role of a gatekeeper keeping an accurate and up-to-date record of all your parents' medications. For a number of reasons, this doesn't happen.

Doctors many times won't ask what other medications are being taken, and too often, our parents don't volunteer what other doctors have prescribed, either.

It is also common for some doctors to renew prescriptions even when there is no longer a need for them. Others prescribe medications to counteract symptoms which may actually be medication-related.

Because of changes in metabolism and organ function that occur as we age, the way our body processes drugs changes. The older we get, the less our body can tolerate drugs. That's why it is important for aging parents to take medications properly.

The problem is millions of seniors fail to take their medications as prescribed or simply quit taking them altogether. This is a big problem, too. The consequences can result in hospitalization or, even worse, end in death.

According to an Associated Press article in July, 2007, about half of the patients with chronic illnesses such as heart disease or asthma skip doses or otherwise muddle up their medication.

Five Ways Parents Damage Their Health and Don't Even Know It

Your mom may not start taking the drug because she doesn't understand how or when to take it. Or, she may simply forget to take it. Pain in her hands from arthritis can keep her from opening the medicine bottles and that can prevent proper medication usage. Or she may simply not be able to read the label!

She may start feeling better and simply toss the rest of the bottle, thinking she doesn't need the medication. Remember when former President Bill Clinton had open heart surgery? He quit taking his cholesterol-lowering statin drug at some point and needed the surgery to avoid a major heart attack.

Statin drugs offer significant heart protection, yet half of those who are prescribed the drug stop taking it within 12 months. Had he stayed on his medication, perhaps heart surgery would not have been necessary.

ELDER FACTS

Adverse drug reaction and non-compliance are responsible for 28% of hospitalizations of the elderly. Source: American Society of Consulting Pharmacists

According to the AP story, poor medication management can add an extra $2,000 per year for each patient in extra doctor visits alone. It is also associated with as many as 40 percent of nursing home admissions, a result that exacts an even higher cost, both financially and emotionally.

The National Council on Patient Information and Education has released a series of videos designed to teach seniors how to take their medications. You might want to check them out at **www.MUSTforSeniors.org.**

A simple way to find out if medications are being taken as prescribed is to look at the date of the prescription on the bottle. Look at how many pills should be taken and how often they should be taken. Next, do some simple math to find out how many pills should be left. Then count the pills remaining in the vial.

If your mom should be taking 30 pills a month, the prescription was filled with 60 pills two months ago, and 19 pills are left, that is a clue to follow up on this medication. Find out why she discontinued its use. Did she do so with the guidance of her physician? Frequently, if seniors have a negative reaction to a medicine, they won't discuss it with their doctor. They may simply decide they aren't going to take it anymore and stop.

Whether the decision to quit taking a drug has a long term effect depends on the medication and how it works inside the body. If your parent has stopped taking a prescribed drug because of a side effect, find out if the doctor can prescribe another drug that eliminates the problem.

If you think your dad is not being forthright about his health, use his prescription labels to guide you. To get an idea of any health issues he may be treating, write down the names of the medicines you find. You can learn what each medicine is used for by visiting your local pharmacist or by checking on the Internet.

The two most authoritative online drug information sites are at **www.Drugs.com** and **www.Medline.gov**. Drugs.com has provided database information to the health care industry for 64 years. Medline.gov is a service of the United States National Library of Medicine and the National Institutes of Health.

Action Notes

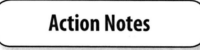

Put what you just read to use. Jot down your ideas, thoughts, and questions as well as any actions you plan to take on the lines below. Have a question for me? E-mail me: Martin@SurvivingEldercare.com. I'm always glad to help.

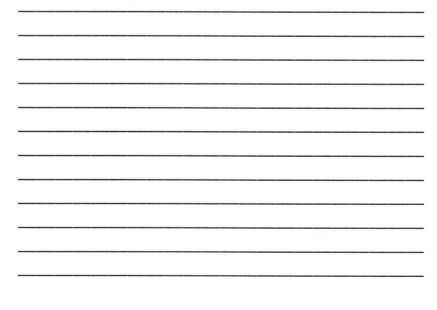

"You can observe a lot just by watching."

~ Yogi Berra

CHAPTER 2

Two Unspoken Rules Of Caregiving

- A Common Stress-Inducing Caregiving Mistake To Avoid
- The Secret To Making Better Decisions Faster With More Confidence
- Big Problems Can Have Small Solutions

If you are involved in caring for your mom or dad for the first time, one of the surprises you will run into is the amount of information you will need to get your arms around.

The amount of information a person needs to run his or her life is stunning. We all learn life management skills as we mature, creating our own system for organizing and controlling the various aspects of our life. Some of us do a better job of it than others, of course. Sooner or later we establish our own pattern and figure out how to adapt to life's pace and demands.

When the care of a parent drops into our lap, life reminds us just how complex it is. So let's take a look at the steps to take when a loved one needs care.

Unspoken Rule #1: Identify the Problem, Then Act

There is a tendency for some caregivers to jump right into the situation. The inclination is to start solving a problem before taking the time to understand what the problem really is.

The very first principle is to know what you need to do before you do it. This means taking the time to assess your loved one's situation and condition along several planes, or dynamics. The dynamics that drive the need for elder care include:

- the health dynamic (both physical and mental health)
- the emotional dynamic
- the financial dynamic
- the social dynamic
- the legal dynamic
- the spiritual dynamic

Each of these areas of life relates to and affects the others in one fashion or another and to different degrees at different times of life. They are the driving forces of living in each of our lives. They are called "dynamics" because each area contains energy and is characterized by continuous change, activity, and progress over time. Every living human being makes decisions every day based on the condition, strength, and direction of each of these dynamics.

The reason you are stepping into your loved one's life — or the reason you feel your intervention is necessary — is because your mom or dad is not progressing well along one of these six dynamics. Assessing a parent's needs will take effort. The process can be intimidating. You will find yourself making better decisions faster with less stress and more confidence if you take the time and keep in mind the following suggestions.

Unspoken Rule #2: To Make Good Decisions, Focus.

Focus is necessary in order to recognize your mom or dad's true condition. It paves the way for decisive action and appropriate solutions. Without focus you disperse your energy, weaken your efforts, and skyrocket your frustration.

I realize focusing is easier said than done when you find yourself dealing with an emotional crisis. But, making good decisions requires an understanding of what is really going on in your parent's life. When you have a lot of confusion swirling around you, the only way to gain mental and emotional stability is to isolate your attention on a single dynamic. Doing so allows you to understand the part of the problem you are trying to solve and rewards you with a perspective you would not otherwise have.

The obvious starting place is health care. Start with the physical issues, because that is what you are going to see first. Doing so allows you to identify specific issues and gives you direction.

For example, your mom has had a couple of falls recently. You go home and notice that your mom has lost a lot of weight and appears to be weak. There are a number of root causes which can lead to falls. Something as simple as her dentures not fitting anymore could be the problem. Her gums hurt when she eats, so she doesn't. Since she is not getting proper nutrition, she is getting weaker. Because she is weak, she falls more often.

Big Problems Can Have Small Solutions

If you only notice that she is falling down, your first thought might be she needs a nursing home. With a little patience and investigation, you may find the solution is as simple as getting her teeth fixed.

Often the solutions can be that easy.

Looking first for a physical cause to a decline makes sense. Doing so is often faster, less expensive, and less stressful for you, your parent, and the rest of the family.

Many seniors will suffer from diminished hearing, vision, or mobility, but it's not a given. If you notice your mom has given up sewing because she no longer sees well enough, get her in for an eye exam. Find out if it is curable eye disorder, such as cataracts.

Sometimes there is nothing that can be done. Sometimes a condition requires surgery. At other times, there can be a simple solution.

A situation with a friend's 94-year-old dad is an example:

Amazingly, my friend's dad uses a bicycle for transportation around his hometown in rural Mississippi. One Friday morning, my friend received a phone call from his 91-year-old mother, telling him his dad had become dizzy while riding to the coffee shop, lost control of his bike, and fell over.

At first, the doctors could not figure out what was causing the dizziness. They checked his medicines for side effects and found nothing. How about his heart and circulatory system? They were fine. High blood pressure? Nope. Everything was okay.

They sent him home with instructions to rest. The dizziness continued.

When my friend arrived from Houston, he realized his dad's hearing seemed worse than the last time he visited. He took him to a hearing specialist.

The ear doctor discovered an unusually large accumulation of wax, deep inside both ears. He cleaned them out and magically restored the man's hearing as well as his balance.

The problem was wax! The solution was to simply have it removed. Today, my friend's dad is back on his bicycle, happily toodling around his hometown.

Just because your mom or dad's mobility, vision, or hearing has diminished, it is not necessarily an indication it is time for you to step in. While it can be part of the normal aging process, it is not always. Still, it's something to note and check out.

There are times you have to act quickly, of course.

If someone is heavily bleeding, actively ill, has a raging fever, has broken a bone, or has plowed the car into the garage, you need to take action. If you live in Los Angeles and you receive a call from your dad's neighbor in Orlando who says your dad has been out wandering the streets the last couple of days, it's time to hop on the next plane. You need to get there as fast as you can.

When a Health Problem Is Bigger Than Originally Thought

Often what appears to be a big problem stems from a small source that is easy to fix. Sometimes the problem is bigger than you originally thought, but good observation enables you to make the most effective lifestyle and therapeutic changes necessary.

A letter from a listener to my "Ask Mr. Eldercare" radio show illustrates this point:

The letter was about his wife. She was having difficulty walking. At first she wrote it off to clumsiness: "Well, I tripped over the carpet." or "I tripped over the step." When she kept falling, he worried there was something deeper that needed medical attention.

She dismissed his suggestions to visit a doctor. When her speech started to slur, he insisted on a trip to her physician. The doctor thought she was suffering from transient ischemic attacks, or TIAs. TIAs are the medical term for "mini-strokes," events that briefly interrupt the flow of blood to the brain. Symptoms typically occur suddenly and disappear within an hour.

When the symptoms continued, they realized the cause was something different. They wanted to come to a mutual understanding of what the problem was. To do that they observed and talked about it. Over several weeks they made notes of their observations. Then, they sought professional help.

The doctors finally determined his wife was suffering from Pick's Disease, a form of dementia. The prognosis for each disease is dramatically different.

TIAs are a warning sign that you are at risk for a future, more debilitating stroke. About 30 percent of those suffering a TIA will have an acute stroke later. Had it been a TIA, by heeding the warning signs, the underlying treatable factors could be addressed to prevent future strokes. With proper treatment, they could minimize the likelihood of more strokes.

Pick's Disease is a different matter.

The outcome is poor. There is no way to cure it. Pick's Disease is a rapidly progressing fatal disease, lasting from two years in some to ten years in others. Eventually, the disease requires 24-hour care and monitoring, at home or in an institutionalized care setting.

The two diseases impact life completely differently. The responses should be completely different, too. By observing, asking the right questions, and getting professional help, this listener was able to better prepare himself for the caregiving journey ahead. Knowing the diagnosis allowed them to plan better for their future, including making important medical, financial, and legal decisions.

If you sense something is wrong, your first step is to identify the problem. It's rare that stepping back and taking a closer look will worsen the situation.

You don't want to jump into your mom or dad's life too quickly to solve a problem. You could find yourself "solving" the wrong problem. The result of acting too soon could make your life more difficult than it needs to be.

Action Notes

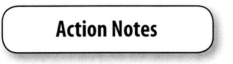

Put what you just read to use. Jot down your ideas, thoughts, and questions as well as any actions you plan to take on the lines below. Have a question for me? E-mail me: Martin@SurvivingEldercare.com. I'm always glad to help.

"We cannot learn from one another until we stop shouting at one another — until we speak quietly enough so that our words can be heard as well as our voices."

~ Richard M. Nixon

CHAPTER 3

How To Turn Resistance Into Cooperation

- Powerful Techniques That Virtually Guarantee Cooperation
- The Hidden Reason Parents Resist Help
- 20 Resistance Melting Ways To Approach Your Parent

What do you do when you have a mom or dad who is not willing to cooperate with you? How do you handle a parent who says: "Everything is fine, honey. I appreciate your concern, but really, I can handle my life. There is nothing to worry about." ?

Geriatric care manager Molly Shomer with the Elder Care Team in Dallas, Texas, refers to this response as, "Chinese water torture." The torturous part is the way worrying about your loved one's safety and well-being pops in and out of your mind every day. It's like a slow, maddening, unpredictable dripping of water on your forehead.

Molly says this:

"You may not get cooperation. You may get denial the first time out. But, as adult children, we have limited authority. All you can really do, assuming mom or dad's situation is not life-threatening or dangerous, is make yourself available and keep coming back to the subject again and again."

It gets extremely frustrating, but it's the only option you really have. Your parents are adults. If they choose to deny their needs and make bad decisions, it is their right.

Molly adds, "Think about it this way: if somebody walks into your mom's house, starts bossing her around and telling her what to do, she is not going to like it very much. She will like it even less if it's her son or daughter, whose diapers she used to change. Like it or not, you may be a successful 63-year-old, but to your mom, you're still her kid."

It is important to realize your parents' perspectives. They have their own needs and concerns and they have the right to make their own decisions — good or bad.

Parent In Denial? A Simple, Powerful Technique That Works

One way to handle your loved one's denial is to reverse the guilt flow. Approach it as, "Would you do it for *me?*" as opposed to, "You need to do this for *you*."

Our parents have spent their lives, in one form or another, sacrificing for their children. It is something they are used to doing. Try phrasing your concern in a way that says, "I need you to do this because it will help me" in some respect. It often gets their cooperation.

By taking this approach you are expressing your emotion about their situation. What you are saying to your mom is, "I am really concerned that you could harm yourself or harm somebody else. I feel bad about this."

It could turn their thinking around.

Rather than figuratively poking a finger on your dad's chest saying, in effect, "Look, you need to make this change!" you are sitting down, holding both his hands and saying, "I have some concerns. Will you help me out?" Doing so "reverses the flow" and frequently works.

Magic Phrases That Melt Resistance

Listen to the way you sound when you talk to your mom. Are you pushy? Condescending? If you find yourself starting sentences with the following phrases, they scream disrespect for your mom or dad's decision making ability:

> "Mom you need to …"
> "Can't you see …"
> "You're being stubborn …"
> "What you need to do is …"

Remember how you reacted when you were a teenager and you heard those same words coming out of her mouth? You didn't like it much, right? You turned a deaf ear and refused to listen.

Your mom won't feel any different now that the roles are reversed.

The solution is to use phrases that are not judgmental. To neutralize a parent's tendency to argue, pay attention to the words you use and how you frame your comments. You will gain a more willing ear by beginning sentences with:

"I'm worried about …"
"I'd feel better if …"
"How do you feel about …"

Your approach will be perceived as less threatening and help you gain a more willing ear.

9 Tips for Talking with Aging Parents

Bring it up gently. Start the dialogue using a recent article in a newspaper or magazine, or the illness of a friend or neighbor. By focusing on someone other than your parents, you are able to ease into the conversation about their current and future needs.

Make it a family affair. While it is typical for one family member to take the lead caregiving role, expect everyone in the family to have an opinion. You need to know what everyone's views are to avoid undermining what you want to accomplish. Your parents' views of their own needs may be different from yours. Your siblings' perspectives may also be different. Get the issues on the table early. Then, work to build support with your parents, your siblings, and other family members who will be involved.

Understand your parents' need to control their own lives. Your parents have a right to make their own decisions. What you are doing is balancing their need for safety with their need for independence. If they feel you are taking away their sense of control over their lives, they will not cooperate.

Be respectful. Your parents have lived a long time. Over that time they have learned quite a bit. They may have sacrificed to give you the life you have. They are facing a period of time full of losses. Many of those losses — physical strength, health, friends, siblings, and financial independence — can't be replaced. Treat them with love, honor, and respect for where they are in life.

Assure them. Let your parents know you are there to gather data about their options and to be made aware of their wishes. Tell them the purpose of the discussion is to help them remain independent as long as possible. Emphasize that your primary interest is to discover what they desire. Framing the talk with these assurances helps them understand the reasons you are addressing such sensitive issues.

Use positive communication skills. Offer options, not advice. Ask your parents for their ideas. Let them know your concerns, but don't dictate what they should think or do. Listen carefully. Use open-ended questions that encourage discussion rather than closed-ended questions which are answered with a "yes" or "no."

Agree to disagree. You may truly believe you know what's best, but your parents may not agree. Remember you are involved in their life by invitation only. Unless their safety is in danger, their wishes take priority.

Educate yourself first, then your parents. Your parents may not know the legal and financial options available to them. The more you know, the better you can guide them. Use the information you learn from this book to become an important resource for them. Our parents' generation prefers to get their information from reading. Give them materials to review. The material itself may open up opportunities for more dialogue.

Reassess when things aren't working out. If the conversations don't go well, it's time to reevaluate what might be going wrong. Do you need to be better informed and have more information handy for their review? Are you coming across in a way that lets your parents understand your true concern and purpose? Maybe you need to pass the task to someone else with whom your parents feel more comfortable talking. It could be another family member such as a sibling, aunt or uncle, their lawyer, doctor, CPA, or minister.

You may increase your chance of success by asking for your parents' input on your own situation. Once they are open to your needs, a parent is more likely to be receptive to discussing theirs. Their guidance can give you an X-ray view of their worries, desires, and attitudes, and give you the opening you need to discuss their care needs with them.

Once the dialogue is open, bring things up naturally from time to time. Focus on one issue at a time. Give your parents the chance to think things over before they respond. The role reversal can feel unnatural and scary for both of you, but having the conversation *now* means you will be better able to handle any crisis that occurs later.

The "Secret Agent" Approach That Gets Uncooperative Parents to Listen

If you have a hard time getting through to your loved one, ask someone that your loved one respects to make the approach. It may be another family member, a brother or sister, an uncle, a church member, the next-door neighbor, a doctor, or a lawyer. The idea is to find someone your mom or dad will listen to who will serve as your "agent."

A Word to the Wise

Before you call for reinforcements, make sure the person you ask for help is on the same page as you. Only then, should you let him or her speak on your behalf. Once your mom or dad agrees, it paves the way for you to step in and help implement the changes. You will be able to move forward without seeming like you are muscling into their life, taking away their independence, and telling them what to do.

In my family, I know my mom will be less resistant to an idea that comes from one of my brothers. He is her favorite. It's just the way it has been ever since I can remember.

With my dad, it is a different story. I have his ear and his respect. He will listen to me, but will turn a deaf ear to any recommendation by another brother of mine, because of their past history.

Sometimes, the single most positive impact you can have on your loved one's life is to simply hang in there.

Sure, you are going to get frustrated, annoyed, and angry. It's part of the territory. Do your best to keep it from showing and don't let that irritation hang around too long. As long as your loved one is coping well enough and is not in personal danger, let it be.

The Hidden Reason Your Mom or Dad Resists Help

Your mom or dad is most likely dealing with deep-seated issues about maintaining control over his or her life. Just because you think they should be helped doesn't necessarily mean they want you to step in and help. Remember, you are involved in your parent's life by invitation only.

Discussing issues of incapacity and making plans for it is likely to be painful for both you and your parents. They are likely to feel insecure, too. It's hard for people who have been self-sufficient to consider dependency. It eats at the very core of their self-esteem.

Be careful about being in too much of a hurry to take your parent under your wing. Trying to take over too much, too fast, can undermine his or her self-esteem.

Overestimating your parent's needs can be destructive to your overall goal. If you assume responsibility for things your parent can still do, the result could be an angry parent, a difficult relationship, and a parent who begins sliding toward depression.

It can be upsetting watching your parent make decisions that lead them down the wrong path. Keep focused on your mom's ability to maintain a quality of life. When the time comes that your help really counts, you may be surprised with the amount she will accept.

You may have to wait for her to reach her "splat point." That's when some critical issue or crisis flattens her perspective against the reality of her life. That's when your loved one says, "Okay, I see there is a problem and I would like you to help me with it."

11 Simple Starter Questions for Aging Parents

If it's hard for you to start that important "conversation" about your mom or dad's future care needs, give these eleven questions a try. Talking about future incapacity is a sensitive subject that may conjure up fears of loss in both you and your parent. Don't tiptoe around the point. If you do, you will never understand how your mom or dad really feels about their care.

Having an honest series of discussions with your mom or dad before a crisis hits allows you to avoid making critical life decisions in the heat of a problem without knowing what care and treatment they prefer.

Remember to take your time. Be understanding and expect some resistance. Over time, you will have a better understanding of your parents' concerns and you will know what steps you can take to make the future less stressful for everyone.

1. Is it okay for me to talk to you about your future financial and care needs?
2. If you should become ill, who do want to handle your finances?
3. If you were to become seriously ill, what level of care or help would you want?
4. Have you compiled a list of your important financial and legal papers? Where is it kept?
5. Have you prepared a list of your medications? Where do you keep it?
6. If you become ill and I need to contact your doctors, where will I find the phone numbers?
7. Would you like to speak to us (the family) about your belongings and how you would like them to be divided, even if you've already specified this in your will?
8. Are there any daily chores you would like us to help you with around the house now? If you become too infirm to handle actions like getting to the doctor, the dentist, or the hairdresser, would you like me to be available to help you?
9. If you can't take care of yourself physically, where would you prefer to live? At home with care? With a family member? In an assisted living facility?
10. What would you do if one of you becomes incapacitated and the other is not?
11. Have you made financial arrangements for either of these eventualities?

Action Notes

Put what you just read to use. Jot down your ideas, thoughts, and questions as well as any actions you plan to take on the lines below. Have a question for me? E-mail me: Martin@SurvivingEldercare.com. I'm always glad to help.

"Fear grows in darkness; if you think there's a bogeyman around, turn on the light."

~ Dorothy Thompson

"We cannot live only for ourselves. A thousand fibers connect us with our fellow men."

~ Herman Melville

CHAPTER 4

Find The Right Help Fast!

- A Source Of Help Most Families Overlook
- Emergency Need? Use These "Quick Connect" Services
- How To Get Instant Help With Every Day Needs In Times Of Crisis

The antidote to worry is confidence. Confidence comes from knowledge. If you find yourself in an emergency situation, you will need to find good information fast. The problem is the need to find information quickly but not knowing where to find it or how to judge the quality of the resources you do find.

The good news is you can access a wide variety of care-giving assistance in most areas of the country. If you are unsure which services your loved one may need, I have provided a quick list below to get you started. In the back of this book, you will find a huge list of organizations. Where available, I have included their phone numbers, street addresses, and web addresses.

You will soon realize this country's health care and elder care support systems are terribly fragmented. The process of gathering information and locating resources can create a great deal of stress and anxiety. There is no simple way to find the specific information you need for your loved one other than rolling up your shirt sleeves and getting to work.

An Unusual, But Very Helpful Source Most Families Overlook

If you are completely without a clue, and either you or your parents belong to a place of worship, contact their senior ministry. Larger churches and synagogues have senior ministries who can help you identify community resources and arrange for volunteers willing to help with everyday tasks.

If that church or synagogue does not have a senior ministry, open up the local yellow pages and find the listings for other churches and synagogues, senior centers, social service organizations, and hospitals in your area.

These groups are already connected to the network of caregiving services in your town. Give each one a call. Let them know why you are calling and the type of help you need. You'll be surprised how quickly you will find direction.

A Quick Resource For A Wide Variety of Aging Issues

Another important first resource is your local Agency on Aging. The AOA is an agency of the U.S. Department of Health and Human Services which offers services that help older persons and their caregivers quickly obtain information and resources on a variety of aging-related topics.

This information will help you become more familiar with the issues affecting your parents, and the services and opportunities available to assist them. Use the white pages to find their number or visit their website at **www.aoa.gov.**

2-1-1 Rapidly Connects To Critical Community Health Services

Another helpful resource available in most major cities is the new 2-1-1 telephone number. It connects you to information about critical health and human services available in the community.

While services available through 211 vary from community to community, the system provides callers with information about, and referrals to, services for everyday needs in times of crisis. Services can include supplying basic human resource needs such as food banks or rent and utility assistance. In addition, these services may include support for older Americans, and those with disabilities, in the form of home health care, adult day care, Meals on Wheels, homemaker services, and respite care.

The network of social agencies constantly changes. Many are non-profit and are staffed by volunteers who may not be as well trained as you would like. Be prepared to run into less than helpful staff, being put on hold, outdated phone numbers, and discontinued programs. To get the information you need, you will need to exercise patience and be persistent.

Be sure to check with your employer, too. Many large corporations offer elder care guidance through an Employee Assistance Program.

The following resources can help you locate information and assistance on a variety of issues at the federal, state, and local levels.

Eldercare Locator — Operated by the U.S. Administration on Aging, this site offers instant connections to services which allow older people to live independently longer. **(www.eldercare.gov)**

Health and Aging Organizations — This is an online, searchable database maintained by the National Institute on Aging. It gives you one-click access to a list of over 250 national organizations that provide help to seniors. **(www.nia.nih.gov/HealthInformation)**

Nursing Home Compare — Located on the Medicare website at **www.Medicare.gov,** this site provides detailed information about the performance of every Medicare and Medicaid certified nursing home in the country.

These organizations change their contact information from time to time. I'm also finding new resources, too. To get the most up-to-date listings, be sure to visit **www.SurvivingEldercare.com.**

Action Notes

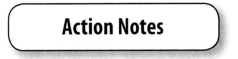

Put what you just read to use. Jot down your ideas, thoughts, and questions as well as any actions you plan to take on the lines below. Have a question for me? E-mail me: Martin@SurvivingEldercare.com. I'm always glad to help.

"The emotions aren't always immediately subject to reason, but they are always immediately subject to action."

~ William James

"Holding on to anger is like grasping a hot coal with the intent of throwing it at someone else; you are the one getting burned."

~ Buddha

CHAPTER 5

Four Ways To Minimize Family Conflict

- The Key To Minimizing Family Conflict
- How To Remove Most Of The Emotion From The Caregiving Equation
- Family members not helping? Do this.
- Two Promises You Should Never Make

As you can see, there are a number of issues that need to be considered if you are an adult child concerned about aging parents. You will deal with two types of problems: the practical issues such as meeting with physicians and arranging for care, and the issues that come up as you and your siblings see the effect aging has on your parents.

Ideally, siblings should share the caregiving burden equally. The reality is much different and often causes a great deal of family tension. That's why it is important to get the other family stakeholders involved and find common ground early in the process.

Whether it is an emergency requiring immediate involvement, or one that allows you time to observe for a while, it is important to get the other family members involved as quickly as possible.

Assuming your family is not estranged getting everyone's observations allows you to see both the situation and the potential solutions through the eyes of others who have a stake in the outcome.

Get Everyone On The Same Page

Use the checklist on page 54 to guide your observations. It allows you and other family members to objectively evaluate your mom or dad's physical, emotional, social and cognitive needs. Using a list like this takes most of the emotion out of the equation allowing a more detached perspective of the safety and health needs to address.

Because each of us sees life differently, expect your family members to have differences of opinion about your loved one's care needs.

If you are the one spending the most time with your mom, you may be the first one to spot something troubling. Many times the changes are so subtle you may not recognize the changing condition.

A brother or sister who sees her less regularly may come for a family visit during Christmas, Thanksgiving, a birthday, or anniversary and see a marked difference. You may write it off as no big deal, but your sibling could be seeing something you have missed.

That is why it is so important to sit down and compare notes. You may hear things that you hadn't even considered.

If you do, ask siblings questions like these:

What are your observations?
How do you interpret what's happening with mom?
What do you think the problem is?

Notice I haven't mentioned anything about hashing out a solution with your siblings at this point. Focus on finding out what the problem is first. If you don't know what the problem is, how can you search for an appropriate solution?

Run Effective Family Meetings: 5 Tips

The best kind of family meeting is run as a business meeting. Somebody takes notes. Everybody gets a chance to speak. Nobody is completely dismissed. It is a chance to sit down and let everyone put concerns on the table. Once they are there, the goal is to pinpoint the most important issues and handle the most pressing ones first.

While it may be difficult, it is important to set aside sibling rivalry. It is not an issue about who is smarter or who is a favorite child. It is a question of deciding what the issues are and agreeing on the matters to solve first. Obtaining an agreement on the three issues that need to be addressed first allows you to establish these as "foundation" issues.

The better able you are to set aside your differences, the better you will be able to work together. The better you can work together, the easier it will be on all parties.

One simple solution that reduces sibling flare-ups is to record the conversation. Having a recorder at the table is somewhat like having an impartial third party at the meeting. It tends to put the lid on family bickering during the meeting and improves the overall decorum of the meeting.

It simplifies note taking, too. Once the meeting is over, get the recording transcribed and distribute copies to everyone in attendance. A good transcriptionist will cost about $45 per hour. You can find them in the yellow pages or by going online to outsourcing companies such as Elance.com and Guru.com.

After reaching some kind of agreement among your siblings regarding the top two or three most important concerns of the group, every other concern goes into the "pending basket" to be dealt with later.

Establishing foundation issues empowers everyone in the group on three fronts:

- It demonstrates the family's ability to reach a consensus on a sensitive topic.
- It focuses everyone's attention on the critical issues to be solved.
- It establishes a precedent for gaining agreement on future matters.

Expect to have dozens of issues surface in your meeting.

Don't expect everyone to agree with your sense of priorities, either. You may find what is at the top of your list is actually less urgent and belongs in the pending file. You won't know until you have worked through it.

The Right Way to Respond to Family Members Who Won't Help.

If you are the "ground zero" caregiver, one secret to keeping stress down is accepting the limitations of your siblings. Each of them has his or her own combination of weaknesses and strengths.

Understand and accept the willingness, abilities, and limitations of each family member. Your task is to see these characteristics clearly. In that way, you can use their strengths the best way possible for you, them, and your aging parent.

Your siblings are the way they are. They have been that way for years. To think they will magically bend a different way because a parent needs help is wishful thinking.

If they haven't changed in forty years what makes you think they will change now?

That brother or sister you could always rely on will be there for you now, too. The one who is emotionally sensitive will still be that way and that jerky brother will still be a jerk. Just because you want them to be there or expect them to help, won't change who they are. Realizing who they are and accepting it makes your life much less stressful in the long run.

Feelings of guilt, anger, and resentment quickly boil to the surface when siblings don't contribute the way you think they should. The best way to handle them is to simply forgive them. The relationship you have with your family and the sibling stress that exists won't go away unless you let go of it first.

Your anger and frustration toward a sibling is like a glowing, hot coal. When you grab it to throw at them, you are the one who gets hurt by it. You simply have to decide if the pain you are causing yourself is really worth it.

Usually, it's not.

That doesn't mean you shouldn't ask for help. On the contrary, you should. You may not always get what you want from the people you want it from. But, if you don't ask, you'll never get it.

If you are a family member, but not at "ground zero," be supportive to the sibling who is. Believe me, it is a lot tougher than it looks.

While you are recognizing your family's limitations, be sure to take stock of your own. The tendency for many lead caregivers is to do it by themselves. The extra stress burden you will be placing on yourself is not good for either you or your loved one.

Never Make These Two Promises To Your Mom or Dad

Be careful not to make promises you might not be able to keep. What may seem like the best solution now may not be the best solution five or ten years down the road. Be careful when you say your mom or dad can live with you or promise to never place your loved one in a nursing home.

You have no idea what their needs will be in times to come or how your circumstances will unfold. Unfulfilled promises can result in feelings of guilt, mistrust, and disappointment.

Parent Care Check List

Indicate whether you have concerns for your parent in any of these areas:

	Yes	No
Balance/falling		
Decision making/judgment		
Dexterity		
Driving		
Eating nutritiously		
Energy level		
Forgetfulness/memory issues		
Hearing		
Overall health		
Socialization		
Strength		
Vision		
Overall ability to live alone safely		

How well does your parent perform each of these activities?

	Can Do Without Help	Needs Stand By Assistance	Unable To Perform
Bathing			
Eating			
Dressing			
Toileting			
Walking			
Personal hygiene			
Getting out of a chair			
Getting out of bed			
Getting in or out of a car			
Preparing meals			
Doing laundry			
Grocery shopping			
Cleaning home/apartment			
Home maintenance			
Driving			
Taking/managing medications			
Using the telephone			
Bill paying			
Keeping track of finances			
Problem solving			

Indicate whether your parent has any of these medical conditions:

	Yes	No
Alzheimer's Disease/Dementia		
Arthritis		
Bladder or bowel condition		
Cancer		
Depression		
Dental Disease		
Diabetes		
Emphysema		
Hearing loss		
Heart Disease		
High Blood Pressure		
Mental illness		
Osteoporosis		
Parkinson's Disease		
Stroke		
Vision loss		
Other		
Other		

Memory — Use this list to indicate your parent's cognitive ability.

	Yes	No
Has noticeable memory problems		
Has trouble learning new tasks or information		
Has difficulty remembering information about friends, family, current events, etc.		
Forgets to turn off the stove, take medication, lock the door, etc.		
Gets confused		
Gets lost		
Unable to tell you what day, month, or year it is		
Wanders during the night		

Social — How would you describe your parent's social circumstances?

	Yes	No
Has lots of friends and sees them regularly		
Has lots of friends but doesn't see them regularly		
Doesn't have many friends		
Is involved in activities outside the home		
Shows less interest in social activities		

Emotional — How would you describe your parent's emotional condition?

	Yes	No
Has lost interest in hobbies		
Seems bored/lonely		
No longer has a sense of humor		
Seems sad/depressed		
Seems impatient		
Seems angry		
Seems stressed		
Has become more suspicious/paranoid		
Is more easily angered or provoked		

Falls — Which of the following describes the condition of your parent?

	Yes	No
Seems unsteady when walking		
Home hazards exist (e.g. throw rugs, cords across floor, hardwood floors, pets, uneven floors/sidewalks, etc.)		
Has had a recent fall		
Has fallen more than twice in 6 months		
Has had a fall resulting in injury		
Should utilize a cane/walker but won't		

Action Notes

Put what you just read to use. Jot down your ideas, thoughts, and questions as well as any actions you plan to take on the lines below. Have a question for me? E-mail me: Martin@SurvivingEldercare.com. I'm always glad to help.

"It's not easy taking my problems one at a time when they refuse to get in line."

~ Ashleigh Brilliant

CHAPTER 6

How To Create Instant Help: The Three Lists Method

- How To Overcome The 5 Factors Limiting How Much Help You Can Give
- Three Steps To Building A Team Of Family, Friends and Strangers You Can Rely On
- The Secret To Getting The Help You Need When You Need It Most

Another important step in helping both you and your mom or dad is setting up both formal and informal support networks consisting of family, friends, volunteers, and professionals.

There is only so much you can do.

To provide the level of care you want to offer, you will need the support of others. The amount of help you can give is limited by your physical strength, your skill levels, time, money, and the relationships you have.

List 1— Caregiving Jobs You Are Willing To Do

You have the right to determine the depth of your caregiving involvement. Take the time to list all the jobs you are willing to do for your parents. Use the list that follows as a guide. Note the things you can't, or don't want to, do.

Some of the caregiving jobs you may face entail:

Laundry	Meal preparation	House cleaning
Grocery shopping	Household maintenance	Running errands
Money management	Bathing	Dressing
Feeding	Toileting	Shaving
Help transferring from bed or chair	Doctor's appointments	Meetings with other advisors
Phone calls to advisors	Managing medications	Hiring aides
Skilled nursing care	Physical therapy	Nutritional counseling
Exercise	Transportation	Companionship
Religious/spiritual involvement	Find an Adult Day Center	Security calls/visits

This list can be broken down further into the "little" jobs that need to be done, such as:

Picking up medicines	Vacuuming a rug	Washing dishes
Sweeping the sidewalk	Shoveling snow	Replacing light bulbs
Minor repairs	Reading to your mom or dad	Researching a service
Raking leaves in the yard	Plant care (inside and out)	Managing aides
Visiting	Making phone calls	Paying bills
Balancing the checkbook	Picking up movies	Washing mom's hair
Helping dad shave	Pet care	Going for a walk

If you have children still at home, also include actions such as "take son to ball practice," and "pick up kids after school." The idea is to list the tasks that confront you every day.

This list will be different over time as both your needs, and those of your mom or dad, change. Keep it updated and handy.

When someone asks, "What can I do to help?" whip out the list and ask them to check off what they feel comfortable doing. If you are not the primary caregiver, you can use this list to offer help to the sibling who is.

A Word to the Wise

When someone asks for help, be ready to say, "Yes." Keep a list of errands or tasks you need help with on hand at all times. When you get overwhelmed and need some time off, don't be afraid to say no to requests from others. Learn to be more assertive and to speak up for yourself.

List #2 — People Who Will Help

Now make a list of all the people you know who might help. Don't prejudge their willingness and summarily leave them off the list. You never know when someone will respond positively to a request. What you are creating here is the beginning of your own personal support system. (See Chapter 7)

Cast a wide net at first. Be sure to include:

- your siblings
- your healthier parent

- aunts and uncles
- children
- step-children
- nieces and nephews
- grandchildren
- cousins
- your neighbors and friends
- your parents' neighbors and friends
- clergy
- church/synagogue members (either yours or those of your parents)
- co-workers

On the list have their names, phone numbers (work, home, and cell), and e-mail addresses.

Now call everyone. Be honest with them. Let them know you may need help and ask if they are willing to assist. Some will agree. Some won't. Some of those who agree now may not be willing or able to follow through later. That's life. The essential step is to prepare your list *before* the need arises.

Make several copies of the list. Keep one with you at all times, another near your phone, a copy in your desk at work and another in your car. In an emergency having this list nearby can save you time and worry. Having the list prepared and readily available *before* a need pops up can be a real life saver.

Joy Loverde in *The Complete Eldercare Planner* suggests giving a copy of this list to every family member as well as your elder. If you are not available, it provides the family a list of others they can call upon for help.

Some of the folks on the list may be willing to help with certain activities but not with others. You want to find out who will pitch in and what tasks they are willing to handle so you can take advantage of this help if and when the need arises.

List #3 — Community Organizations

Once you have family and friends in place, check out your community to see what free or low cost services are available. Some of the community groups listed below may provide volunteers willing to help out with various needs. Give them a call to find out what they can provide.

- Community centers
- Local Agency on Aging
- Fraternal orders
- Senior groups at Churches/Synagogues
- Charities
- Neighborhood groups
- Women's groups
- Advocacy groups
- Youth groups
- United Way agencies
- Senior's organizations
- Veteran's organizations
- Support groups
- Family service organizations

If the organization you call cannot supply the help you need, they may be able to refer you to another organization that can. Be sure to ask.

ELDER FACTS

Men are taking responsibility for the same everyday tasks as women, including grocery shopping, managing medications, and transportation. Women are more involved in personal care, such as bathing, dressing, and toileting. Source: The MetLife Study of Sons at Work (June 2003)

As with the list of potential helpers (List #2), write down the name of the organization, their contact number, and the position of the person who can help you along with that person's name.

The person's position is important because the person you speak with now may not be there when you call later. Knowing the position allows you to get directly to the right person when you need help.

Action Notes

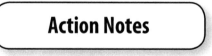

Put what you just read to use. Jot down your ideas, thoughts, and questions as well as any actions you plan to take on the lines below. Have a question for me? E-mail me: Martin@SurvivingEldercare.com. I'm always glad to help.

____

____

"May God give you ...
For every storm a rainbow, for every tear a smile,
for every care a promise and a blessing in each
trial. For every problem life sends, a faithful
friend to share, for every sigh a sweet song
and an answer for each prayer."

~ Irish Blessing Quote

CHAPTER 7

The Secret Weapon Of Successful Family Caregivers

- The Secret To A Personal Support System That Really Works
- Three Powerful Reasons Why You Need A Support System
- How To Create A Genuine Support System Virtually Overnight

It does not matter how much you love your parents; it will get to be too much for you if you don't have a personal support system.

The most successful caregiving adult children have well established social support systems in place. A support system makes the caregiving burden easier to share and prevents the all too common problems of caregiver burn-out, depression, and illness.

How A Personal Support System Differs From a Support Group

A support group is a structured entity typically run by a hospital, mental health organization, or a disease related association such as the Alzheimer's Association or the Cancer Society. A personal support network consists of people you know and can turn to for support, help, relaxation, or diversion. These are the people you can turn to during a crisis.

Having access to a diverse and supportive group helps you cope better with hard times and serves as an effective psychological buffer against stress and depression.

The more you become involved in providing care to an aging parent, the easier it is to become isolated, overwhelmed and overstressed.

Why A Support System Works So Well

Having a network of friends, family, and professionals acts as both an emotional safety net to catch you when you lose your balance, and a compass to keep you pointed in the right direction.

> ***ELDER FACTS***
>
> *Nearly seven out of ten (69%) family caregivers spend less time with family and friends since becoming caregivers. Source: Evercare Study of Caregivers in Decline: A Close-Up Look at the Health Risks of Caring for a Loved One (www.evercarehealthplans.com, 2006)*

Your personal support system may consist of siblings, who can help relieve some of your duties, clergy, who can give you spiritual advice, and religious groups, who can volunteer to help relieve some of your burden.

There are also public programs that are intended to be supportive of those who are caring for the elderly. Social workers and adult day care centers are among the most useful in helping to provide the support you will need.

Good friends can be particularly helpful.

They can be there for you to talk to and give you a shoulder to cry on. Having a "willing ear" in troubling times is good for your overall mental well-being. Sometimes you just need to vent! Your support team will sometimes point out solutions you can't see because you are too close to the problem.

Remember to add your parents' doctors as key members of your support network. Don't be afraid to phone your parents' doctors anytime you are unsure about something and need their help.

Take a few minutes now to write a list of those you know you can add to your support system. Then let them know you need their help. You will be pleasantly surprised by how much cooperation you get.

Instantly Tap Into Thousands Of Caregivers Any Time Day or Night

Thanks to the Internet, you can tap into literally thousands of people facing similar caregiving issues through online support groups. One of the best is moderated by Denise Brown at **www.caregiving.com.** You can find others by searching online for "online support groups." You will find hundreds through that search.

Online support groups are handy for a number of reasons.

The first is you never have to leave your home. You can find advice, direction, and emotional support 24-hours a day, seven days a week, without having to take off your fuzzy slippers and without having to get dressed up. There is no need to fix your hair. There is no need to get in your car to drive somewhere.

They are a convenient way to connect with, and build relationships with other caregivers all over the country who understand what you are facing. It allows you to easily connect to a group that has similar experiences, concerns, and needs.

Knowing you can rely on a supportive group promotes a sense of belonging and improves your sense of self worth. Having a support system in place, and using it, pays incredible dividends for both you and your loved one.

Action Notes

Put what you just read to use. Jot down your ideas, thoughts, and questions as well as any actions you plan to take on the lines below. Have a question for me? E-mail me: Martin@SurvivingEldercare.com. I'm always glad to help.

"Money doesn't talk, it swears."

~ Bob Dylan

CHAPTER 8

Money Pressures And How To Deal With Them

- A Simple Step That Frees Emotion From Money Discussions
- Key Financial Questions Every Parent Should Answer
- The Embarrassing Financial Problem Parents Hate To Reveal

The financial side of eldercare can get pretty sticky. Aside from sex, no subject is more emotional than money. This is particularly true with elderly parents.

Our parents suffered through the trying times of the depression. Their view of money is different than ours. So is their emotional relationship with it. While we are generally open about financial matters, they are not.

When they grew up, it was not something they talked about. If your parents are open about their financial situation, consider it a blessing. If not, and you don't want to be caught off guard later, it is wise to bring up the subject.

Money can be a major point of pressure for adult children and their elderly parents. A key financial issue is their ability to meet current expenses. Another is how well they manage their resources to meet those expenses tomorrow and the next day.

Another is a discussion of debts.

An Embarrassing Financial Problem Your Parents May Be Hiding

Massive debt accumulation is a growing problem among our parents' generation. With the increasing costs of food, utilities, and prescription drugs pushing against fixed income, tens of thousands of seniors turn to their credit cards. Sometimes it is for essentials such as food and medicine. Many times seniors rely on credit cards to continue their lifestyle without tipping off their kids.

I see it all too frequently.

Three recent clients were suffering with crushing credit card debt. One owed $50,000. Another owed $90,000. The third owed a crushing debt of $275,000 on a $300,000 house and another $170,000 in debts to a variety of creditors. The youngest was 72. The oldest was 83.

Debt that high, that late in life, is hard to imagine, isn't it? Yet, it is happening right under our noses with increasing regularity. Is your mom or dad in the same situation?

If so, they may be understandably reluctant to let you know. On the other hand, they may actually be relieved to get some help.

ELDER FACTS

For Americans between the ages of 65 and 69, credit card debt exploded 271% between 1994 and 2004. Seniors use credit cards to afford doctor's visits, prescription drugs and household emergencies when they lack sufficient income and savings. Source: BCS Alliance.com

How To Take The Emotion Out Of Financial Discussions

I recommend taking the emotion out of the conversation by using the services of a professional financial planner.

Financial planning is not just for the wealthy. In fact, it is more important for those who have limited resources. Those who are less well off have less room for financial mistakes.

Your parents might be wondering about their financial stability but they may find it difficult to talk about it. The longer you wait, the fewer choices you will have.

Finding a good one may take some foot work and attentive persistence. That's because the use of the term "financial planner" is not well regulated. Most planners are generalists who look at a person's overall finances. Skilled financial planners make sure you cover all the bases —

- cash flow
- asset allocation
- debt management
- insurance
- government benefits
- estate distribution

The arena of elder care financial planning is specialized so you will want to find a planner who understands issues specific to the elderly like long term care insurance, Medicare, Medicaid and Veteran's benefits, is patient and knows how to communicate with seniors.

The best place to start is with friends, family, fellow employees, church members, or other advisors, such as attorneys and accountants.

Often professional advisors have direct experience with financial planners who are skilled in working with senior issues. Let me add a word of caution here: recommendations, even from professionals you trust are not risk free. The advisor making the recommendation may not have intimate knowledge of the planner's skills.

It's still your responsibility to verify credentials and skill levels. Gather the names of 3 to 5 planners then set up a 20-30 minute interview with each one. Yes, it will take some time, but the risks are significant. You want to find someone who puts your parents' needs first, is willing to invest time learning about their needs and talks in terms you can understand.

You can also check with the following organizations:

American Institute of Certified Public Accountants
888-777-0077 — **www.aicpa.org**

Financial Planning Association
800-322-4237 — **www.fpanet.org**

National Association of Personal Financial Advisers
888-333-6659 — **www.napfa.org**

Remind your parents that if anything happens to them, the burden of managing their finances will fall to you and your siblings. Being open now will make it much easier to follow their wishes and will help ensure they are as comfortable as possible in the future.

18 Basic Financial Questions Every Parent Should Answer

Here is a rundown of the critical financial questions it would be helpful to have answered:

1. What is your parents' financial status (assets, debts, income, and expenses)?
2. What is the current market value of their investments?
3. What is the value of their home?
4. Is the home mortgaged? How much is owed?
5. Where do your parents keep their financial records?
6. What steps have they taken, if any, to minimize estate taxes?
7. Are they receiving all the Social Security benefits to which they are entitled?
8. Are they eligible for Medicare? In which programs have they enrolled?
9. What are the provisions of their pension plans?
10. What benefits are provided through their medical and hospital insurance? Is this adequate?
11. Do they have long term care insurance? Where is the policy kept?
12. What life insurance plans do they have? Where are those policies?
13. What are their monthly budget requirements?
14. Are they able to meet their monthly financial needs?

15. How much debt do they have?
16. Are income taxes fully paid?
17. Have they made funeral arrangements? With whom? Have they fully paid for these arrangements?
18. How do you contact their attorney, tax accountant, and financial consultant?

Your parents may be affronted by these types of questions. In order to avoid offending them, get their permission beforehand to ask them. A simple, "Dad, I'd like to ask a few questions about your finances, is that okay?" can open the door to this very important topic.

Again, reassurance is important to a free and open exchange of information. To get their cooperation, it's essential your mom or dad realize your primary concern is their comfort and security. Let them know you understand that helping them make good decisions does not necessarily mean making those decisions for them.

Action Notes

Put what you just read to use. Jot down your ideas, thoughts, and questions as well as any actions you plan to take on the lines below. Have a question for me? E-mail me: Martin@SurvivingEldercare.com. I'm always glad to help.

"Understanding brings control."

~ Bonewitz

"I do not seek. I find."

~ Pablo Picasso

CHAPTER 9

What Long Term Care Really Costs: How To Afford It

- **The Five Key Factors Of Care Cost**
- **Hidden Financial Dangers For Caregivers**
- **Where To Find Money To Pay For Care**

What exactly do we mean by "long term care?"

Most people think “nursing home” when they hear the phrase “long term care.” Long term care is much more than that. It includes both medical and non-medical care to help people meet their personal and health needs.

The term “long term care” refers to a broad range of health and support services delivered to someone who is chronically ill, frail, or disabled. The majority of these services involve personal care — assistance with activities of daily living such as eating, dressing, walking, bathing, and going to the bathroom.

Long term care services can be delivered:

- at home
- in a hospital
- in the community

- in assisted living arrangements
- or in nursing homes (also known as skilled nursing facilities).

Most long term care is not provided in an institutionalized setting but at home with the help of family and friends.

As the care and support needs of your parents increase, you will find the services of paid care providers becomes necessary for three reasons:

1) to supplement the care you can give
2) to get relief from the daily stress of caregiving
3) to provide the higher levels of care demanded by their declining health

The need to consider an assisted living community or a nursing home typically occurs when it is no longer safe or practical to provide care at home.

The cost of long term care varies with the type and amount of care required, the provider you select, and the area of the country where you live.

The average costs in the United States (in 2007) were:

- $181/day for a semi-private room in a nursing home
- $205/day for a private room in a nursing home

- $2,714/month for care in an Assisted Living Facility (for a one bedroom unit)
- $25/hour for a Home Health Aide
- $17/hour for Homemaker Services
- $61/day for care in an Adult Day Health Care Center

The critical question is: where will you find the money to pay such high costs?

To make the best decisions about how to pay for long term care, you need to understand what services cost, which public programs your parents may qualify for, what these public programs cover, the private financing options available, and which options will work best for your circumstances.

Use the explanations that follow as a guide. This list is by no means exhaustive but you will have a better idea where to look to find money to pay for care. Where applicable, I have indicated which programs have eligibility requirements and noted the risk of running out of funds provided by each source.

(If you have not done so already, I encourage you to register your ownership of this book by visiting **www.SurvivingEldercare.com** so you can access a comprehensive list of resources available only to registered readers. As more resources become available, or as contact information changes, I will update the list for you.)

Your Parents' Personal Savings

If your parents have sufficient income and assets, they will begin paying for care on their own. Most seniors do. It's known as "self-insuring." Personal resources include all assets convertible to cash such as:

- Checking, savings, and money market accounts
- Certificates of Deposit
- Stocks, bonds, U.S. Savings Bonds, and mutual funds
- Real estate, including their home
- Mineral interests
- Annuities
- Cash value of life insurance policies
- Individual Retirement Accounts (IRAs)
- 401k and 403b plans
- Pension and other retirement income

Paying for long term care out of personal income and resources can become a challenge because of the high costs involved. Simply put, your parents' assets and income may not be enough to meet the necessary costs of care.

Advantages of Using Your Parents' Personal Savings and Income:

- Parents enjoy sense of self-sufficiency
- Privacy: no need to reveal finances to third parties
- Freedom to select level of care
- Freedom to select site of care
- Freedom to select care provider

Disadvantages of Using Your Parents' Personal Savings and Income:

- Inadequacy of available funds
- Lower quality and frequency of care
- Penalties paid on liquidation of certain assets
- May leave no legacy to heirs

Family Financial Support and Caregiving

The fact that you are reading this book proves the important role of support by friends and family in paying for a parent's long term care needs.

A 2007 study by Evercare, a leading health care coordination program, and the National Alliance of Caregiving, a leading national research authority on caregiving, found just how costly that support can become.

According to their research, "Caregivers — What They Spend, What They Sacrifice," the typical family caregiver spent about $5,000 per year. Money is spent for:

- Household goods
- Food
- Meals
- Travel and transportation
- Prescription drugs
- Insurance co-payments
- Medical equipment
- Medical supplies
- Clothing

The amount spent was greater than the caregivers' annual spending on their health care and entertainment combined. Surprisingly, lower income caregiving households spent about the same as higher earning households.

Understandably, if you are a long distance caregiver, you will spend more: $8,728. Caregivers living with their loved one spent $5,885. Those who cared for a loved one less than 60 minutes away spent $4,570.

Caregivers sacrifice more than money.

They also contribute a lot of time. According to the Evercare story, more than half did not work and nearly 40 percent said they either had to cut back on their work hours or quit their employment.

When you and other family members willingly devote time and energy to provide care to a parent, it greatly reduces the cost to your parents, but it significantly increases your costs, sometimes in ways you won't realize at first.

The most obvious personal costs are:

- spending less on hobbies, vacations, and leisure activities
- saving less or eliminating savings for college
- cutting back on clothing expenses
- curbing utility use (natural gas, electricity and cell phones)
- pruning transportation costs
- eating up your savings

Among the less obvious costs is the increase in medical insurance costs if you are no longer covered by your employer. You will either be forced to pay the much higher COBRA rates or, worse yet, be without insurance altogether.

Reducing the number of hours of employment means you have less money to invest in your company 401k/403b plans, which means you will have less retirement financial security. If your employer offers a pension plan, you lose employment credits and that reduces your ultimate retirement income.

ELDER FACTS

Caregiving has even resulted in individuals turning down promotions and assignments, or taking early retirement, costing nearly $659,000 over their lifetime in lost wages, social security, and pension contributions. Source: The MetLife Juggling Act Study of 1999

The financial issues also create a hidden and potentially dangerous ripple effect on your emotional and physical health.

According to the Evercare/National Alliance of Caregiving Study, caregivers suffer an increased level of anxiety. They have difficulty sleeping. They worry about their financial situation. They also experience depression or hopelessness and declines in physical health.

Stress is not good for your health, as you will see in Chapter 12, "Six Rules For Avoiding Caregiver Burnout." While stress is part of the caregiving equation, there are steps you can take to minimize its negative effects.

It is difficult to predict how much care your mom or dad will need. What you can reasonably foresee is the longer care is needed, the more expensive it will become. If your parents have limited resources, you could end up paying for some of it out of your personal finances.

That is why it is crucial to figure out the financial alternatives you have. You can then use those for which your parent qualifies to pay as much of the long term care costs as possible.

Long Term Care Insurance

Long term care insurance is provided by private insurance carriers. This coverage helps pay for both skilled and non-skilled care. Coverage varies widely. Some policies cover care only in a nursing home. Others will cover a broader list of services such as medical equipment, adult day care centers, assisted living communities and nursing homes.

Insurance companies require applicants to be in fairly good health to qualify for coverage. If your mom or dad is already ill and not currently covered by long term care insurance, coverage now is not likely.

If your mom or dad has long term care insurance in place, check the policy for coverage details and call the company for an explanation of benefits.

When Are Long Term Care Benefits Paid?

It is important to understand how benefits are paid from a long term care policy. Insurance companies determine when to pay for a service using objective measures spelled out in the contract. These are referred to as "benefit triggers." Typically, insurance companies activate benefits on the basis of a loss of at least two activities of daily living (ADLs) and cognitive impairment.

The agreement will state how and when the insurance company will pay benefits. Long term care insurance typically pays back costs incurred for services covered under the contract up to a pre-set limit. Some policies simply provide a pre-set daily cash amount when you meet the "benefit trigger" whether you have paid for services or not.

Benefits start after a period of time has elapsed. This is known as the "elimination period." The elimination period is a number of days that must pass after a benefit trigger but before the insurer reimburses for services.

Think of it as you would the deductible on your car insurance. Rather than a dollar amount, it is expressed as a period of time. During the elimination period, your parent must pay for services received. In some cases, other insurance, such as Medicare and Medicare supplements, will pick up those costs.

Advantages to Having Long Term Care Insurance

- Protects against long term care costs
- Preserves choices in care — you choose the type of service
- Customizes care based on your financial and social situation
- Preserves other financial assets
- Increases potential for leaving a legacy to your family

Disadvantages to Having Long Term Care Insurance

- If it is not purchased from a reputable company, you may not receive the protection anticipated
- Rising costs of care may exceed benefits paid under the policy
- If underinsured, you may have to use other assets to pay for some services
- Policy may limit benefits to nursing homes and provide no coverage in the home or assisted living communities

A Surprising Source of Long Term Care Financial Relief

You may be surprised to know your mom or dad's life insurance policies could provide funding for their long term care needs. Many policies will allow them to access the policy values while they are still alive.

If your mom or dad has a life insurance policy and the purpose for which it was bought no longer exists, your parent may be able to sell it to raise cash to pay long term care costs. For example, say your divorced or widowed dad bought a policy to provide income protection for your mom, or acquired a policy to protect a business interest that no longer exists. He has three possible means of converting the policy to fund long term care expenses.

Life Settlements

Using what is known as a “life settlement,” the policy is sold to a third party for the policy’s present value. The price paid is a multiple of the cash value available from the insurance carrier but is less than the death benefit.

Generally, the owner of the policy must be over the age of 65 and not terminally or chronically ill. The purchaser is responsible for all future premium payments and becomes the new beneficiary of the policy.

Sale proceeds have no restrictions. They can be used for any purpose including regular living expenses, paying the premiums for long term care insurance, or paying directly for long term care help.

For the most part, life settlements are best used by high net worth individuals. There are tax consequences involved with a life settlement transaction. Be sure to get advice from a lawyer, CPA, or financial advisor who has experience dealing with these agreements.

Advantages of Using a Life Settlement

- Provides cash to pay for care needs
- Generates cash above the living values offered by the issuing company
- Protects other savings and investments

Disadvantages of Using a Life Settlement

- They are highly complex financial transactions
- Your state may not regulate life settlement transactions
- Proceeds are taxable
- Little or no death benefit may be left for survivors/heirs
- Funds received may not cover all long term care costs

Viatical Settlements

A Viatical settlement (from the Latin word meaning "money for a journey") is similar to a life settlement with some important differences.

Just as with a life settlement, your parents can sell a life insurance policy to a third party. The money has no restrictions and can be used for any purpose, including paying for care. A big difference between life settlements and Viatical settlements is that Viatical settlements are only available to those who are terminally ill. Generally, this means the insured person's life expectancy is two years or less.

The insured person will receive between 50 and 80 percent of the policy's death benefit, based on life expectancy (see chart below). The Viatical company becomes the new owner and beneficiary of the policy and is responsible for premium payments. At death, the Viatical company receives the full death benefit.

Unlike taxation on life settlements, money paid from a Viatical settlement is generally tax-free. As with life settlements, the solicitation and sale of Viatical agreements is unregulated in some states. Be sure to protect yourself by checking with your state's Attorney General's office or your state's Departmentof Insurance before making a final decision to use this approach to paying for long term care. You might also want the advice of an attorney who is familiar with Viatical settlements.

Advantages of Using Viatical Settlements

- Money is received instantly
- Provides a valuable asset if your parent does not have long term care insurance
- Relief from premium payments
- Payments may be tax free
- Does not require proof of health

Disadvantages of Using Viatical Settlements

- Insured must be terminally ill with a life expectancy of two years or less
- Should your parent live longer than two years, long term care needs may exceed the benefit received
- Only about 50 percent of applicants are approved
- Heirs will not receive any part of the death benefit

The National Association of Insurance Commissioners (NAIC) has established guidelines regarding appropriate amounts for Viatical settlements. These amounts are based on life expectancy as shown here:

Life Expectancy	Benefit
1-6 months	80%
6-12 months	70%
12-18 months	65%
18-24 months	60%
Over 24 months	50%

Accelerated Death Benefits

While practices vary from company to company, accelerated death benefits take the form of a loan against the death benefit.

Many life insurance companies offer an "accelerated death benefit" option. An accelerated death benefit (ADB) can provide a significant cash advance of the death benefit while the insured is still living. Advances can be as high as 80 percent.

In some cases this is only available as a rider. The rider may be provided free of charge by the insurance company or it may require a modest premium payment. The benefit may not be mentioned in older policies, but many companies will make it available if it is requested. It pays to ask even if it is not mentioned in the policy.

This benefit is available if your mom or dad has a terminal illness, requires permanent nursing home placement, or is incapable of performing activities of daily living (eating, dressing, bathing, transferring, and using the bathroom).

When payments are received from an ADB policy prior to death, the amount you receive is subtracted — with interest — from the amount otherwise payable to the policy beneficiaries when the insured dies.

Advantages of Using Accelerated Death Benefits for Long Term Care Costs

- Helps pay for long term care needs
- Preserves other savings and investments
- Leaves a legacy to heirs
- Usually low cost (or no cost) for the rider

Disadvantages of Using Accelerated Death Benefits for Long Term Care Costs

- Premiums must continue being paid
- Only available for a terminal illness, if a nursing home is needed, or if the insured is unable to perform the activities of daily living
- May not pay enough to cover all long term care costs

Action Notes

Put what you just read to use. Jot down your ideas, thoughts, and questions as well as any actions you plan to take on the lines below. Have a question for me? E-mail me: Martin@SurvivingEldercare.com. I'm always glad to help.

"Research serves to make building stones
out of stumbling blocks."

~ Arthur D. Little

CHAPTER 10

Smart Ways To Tap Home Equity

- When To Use Home Equity To Pay For Care
- Five Arguments For Selling The House; Four Reasons Not To
- Powerful Reasons To Consider A Sale-Leaseback
- The Truth About Reverse Mortgages

For most retired Americans, their home is their greatest financial asset. It is also one of their most important emotional assets. By the time they reach the age when they need long term care, the mortgage is substantially reduced or completely paid. As the mortgage is reduced, the equity (the difference between the amount owed and the market value) grows.

Is it wise to use the home to pay for long term care costs? It depends. Because so much money can be tied up in the equity of your parents' home, it pays to understand how you can free it up for care needs.

Choosing to tap into home equity can be a big decision. There are many emotional, practical, and financial factors to consider including:

- Is it smarter to sell the house or to take out a home loan? You will need to balance health and safety issues with the desire to stay in familiar surroundings.
- If the decision is to stay at home, and you decide to borrow, what are the benefits and risks that come with different types of home loans?
- How will the decision to keep the home, sell it, or borrow against it, affect your mom or dad's eligibility for public programs such as Medicare, Medicaid, and Veterans assistance, should they be needed?

The key is to evaluate how to use the equity in the home as part of an overall plan. There are three ways the equity in your parents' home can be used for care expenses:

1. Sell the home outright
2. Buy the home from your parents and lease it back to them
3. Use a reverse mortgage

Should You Sell The Home?

One of the most difficult decisions your parents will face is when it is time to consider their housing needs. A house that was ideal thirty years ago may now be too difficult to maintain.

Bernadine, a 76-year-old client, recently placed her husband in a nursing home after 55 years of marriage. The six bedroom home in which they raised their children had grown too large for her to keep clean on her own. The cost of keeping her husband at home with care for seven years had drained their bank accounts of their savings. Her limited social security payment would barely cover the cost of utilities and her medications.

She wisely decided to sell the house so she could move into an apartment. It would be easier for her to maintain and it would free up much needed capital for her needs. Plus, she would be closer to her children.

Two other elderly clients — Charlie, 82 and his wife Helena, 79 — lived on twenty acres in a small rural area about two hours from Houston. Neither one could drive any longer. Both needed care and they were becoming increasingly isolated because the area where they lived had little public transportation.

When Helena fell off the porch and broke her hip, it became clear both of them needed to be closer to better medical facilities and care services. Much to the relief of their two daughters, they made the difficult decision to sell the place and move into an independent retirement community in Houston near their daughters.

The proceeds from the sale of the property appear to be sufficient to pay for their care needs for the rest of their lives. Also, the daughters feel more secure now that their parents are close enough to look after regularly.

Another reason you might want to sell the home is if the neighborhood is deteriorating and personal safety is a concern.

Advantages of Selling the Home for Long Term Care Needs

- Improved lifestyle
- New living arrangements could be less expensive
- Equity can be used to pay for care needs
- Capital gains may be exempt for homeowners over 55 if the home was their principal residence in two of the five years preceding the sale — check with a tax advisor

Disadvantages of Selling the Home for Long Term Care Needs

- The home will not be available to pass on as a legacy
- Proceeds may be insufficient to pay for long term care needs
- The sale may create a capital gain tax — check with a tax advisor
- Proceeds may prevent eligibility for some public programs

Key Considerations In Arranging A Sale-Leaseback

If moving is not a good option, you might consider buying the home from your parents as an investment and renting it back to them. This arrangement is called a sale-leaseback. You provide much needed liquidity to your parents and you get the tax advantages of owning rental property. Your parents no longer need to worry about maintenance or paying property taxes. As the homeowner, those are now your responsibility.

Your mom or dad can use the proceeds from the home sale any way they like. As the investor, you take over the property once your parent stops living there. If you don't have the funds or the credit to buy the house, you may be able to find a home investor willing to enter into a sale-leaseback agreement.

Advantages to Using a Sale-Leaseback for Long Term Care Needs

- Frees up important resources for long term care expenses
- Allows parents to stay in familiar surroundings
- Relieves parents from the expense of home maintenance and tax payments
- Capital gains may be exempt for homeowners over 55 if the home was their principal residence in two of the five preceding years preceding the sale — check with a tax advisor

Disadvantages to Using a Sale-Leaseback for Long Term Care Needs

- The new owner gets the home — if it's not a family member, the home does not stay in the family

- The sale may create a capital gains tax — check with a tax advisor
- Proceeds may prevent eligibility for some public programs

When A Reverse Mortgage Makes Sense

If you expect your parents to live in their current home for several years, a reverse mortgage may be worth considering. It is a special kind of home equity loan that allows them to use the equity built up over the years to pay the cost of care or for any other purpose they decide.

With a reverse mortgage, your mom or dad receive cash against the value of their home without selling it. They have the choice of receiving the money in a lump-sum payment, as a series of monthly payments, or as a line of credit. There are no restrictions on how they use reverse mortgage funds.

Reverse mortgages are available to homeowners who are 62 and older. Unlike a traditional mortgage, borrowers are not required to provide an income or credit history to qualify.

No monthly payments are required. Instead, the amount owed, based on loan payouts and interest on the loan, accumulates over time. It is not necessary to repay the loan as long as your mom or dad lives in the home. The loan becomes due when the last borrower (such as the remaining spouse) dies, sells the home, or permanently moves out of it.

Your parent continues to live in the home and retain title and ownership of it. They are still responsible for taxes, hazard insurance, and home repairs. The funds from a reverse mortgage are non-taxable and do not affect Social Security or Medicare benefits. In some cases, the proceeds may impact eligibility for Medicaid benefits.

> ***ELDER FACTS***
>
> *A reverse mortgage converts equity in the home into monthly streams of income, a line of credit or a lump sum which is repaid when the owner no longer occupies the home. Home owners age 62 and older are eligible. An income is not required to qualify nor is there a required monthly payment.*

There are three types of reverse mortgages:

- Home Equity Conversion Mortgage (HECM) — This program is offered by the Department of Housing and Urban Development (HUD) and is insured by the FHA. HECMs are the most popular reverse mortgages, representing about 90 percent of the market.

- Fannie Mae Home Keeper Loan — Borrowers may receive more cash from these loans than from HECMs because the loan limit for these loans is higher.
- Financial Freedom Cash Account Loans — These loans are designed for seniors who own expensive homes.

Most people get a reverse mortgage through a mortgage lender. Some credit unions and banks, along with state and local housing agencies, may also offer these loans.

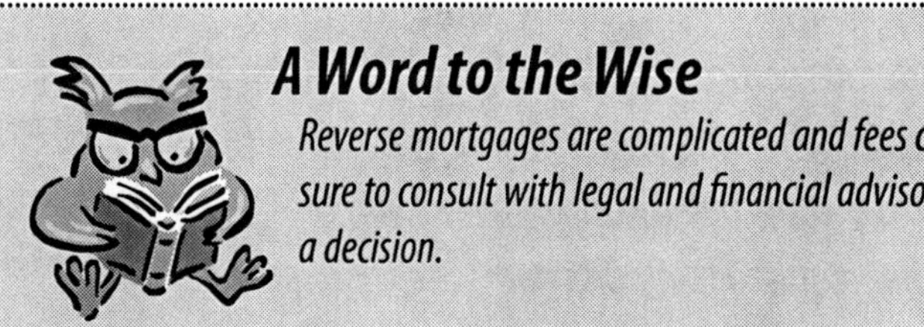

A Word to the Wise

Reverse mortgages are complicated and fees can be high. Be sure to consult with legal and financial advisors before making a decision.

Your parents can use the funds received from a reverse mortgage to pay for a wide array of in-home and community services, and other expenses, such as home repairs and transportation, which may make it safer and more comfortable for them to live at home. They can also use the funds to purchase long term care insurance if they are healthy enough to qualify.

As with all significant financial transactions, it is a good idea to get the advice of a skilled financial advisor or CPA before making a final decision.

Advantages of Using a Reverse Mortgage to Pay Care Costs

- Retains ownership of home
- No income or health requirements to qualify
- Choice of how money is received
- No limitations on how money is used
- Increases monthly cash flow
- Money is received tax-free
- Protects other savings and investments

Disadvantages of Using a Reverse Mortgage to Pay Care Costs

- Costs of long term care may exceed amounts borrowed
- If all proceeds are used for care, may leave no inheritance for heirs
- Taxes, insurance, and maintenance costs must still be paid
- Proceeds may interfere with eligibility for some public programs

How Does a Reverse Mortgage Compare with a Conventional Mortgage?

	Conventional Mortgage	**Reverse Mortgage**
Purpose:	To purchase a home.	To get cash from home equity.
At the time of closing:	You owe a lot and have little equity in the home.	You owe little and have a lot of equity in the home.
During the loan:	• You *make* monthly payments • The loan balance decreases • Your equity grows	• You *receive* payments (as a lump sum, monthly payment, or line of credit) • The loan balance rises. • Your equity decreases
At the end of the loan:	You owe nothing. You have substantial equity in the home.	You may owe a large amount. You may have little or no equity in the home.
Closing costs:	Based on the amount of the loan. Can be financed as part of the loan.	Based on appraised value of the home. Can be financed as part of the loan.
In short ...	Falling debt Rising equity	Rising debt Falling equity

ELDER FACTS

The amount you can borrow on a reverse mortgage varies with age, current interest rate, loan fees, the home's market value and program mortgage limits for your area. The greater the value of the home, the older the owner and the lower the interest, the more you can borrow.

Action Notes

Put what you just read to use. Jot down your ideas, thoughts, and questions as well as any actions you plan to take on the lines below. Have a question for me? E-mail me: Martin@SurvivingEldercare.com. I'm always glad to help.

"The beginning of knowledge is the discovery of something we do not understand."

~ Frank Herbert

CHAPTER 11

But I Thought Medicare Paid For That!

- **Oops! The Disconnect Between Medicare And Long Term Care Costs**
- **Medicaid Could Be The Answer For You**
- **Nearly Secret Program For Veterans Who Need Solutions To High Care Costs**

Many people believe they can rely on Medicare to pay for long term care services. Don't bank on it. Medicare only pays for long term care if your loved one requires skilled services or recuperative care, and only for a short period of time. It will not cover custodial care (assistance with activities of daily living), which is the largest part of long term care.

Medicare is a federal program for those who are 65 and older. It only covers medically necessary care. It focuses on acute medical care (doctor visits and hospital stays) and short term services for conditions that are expected to improve.

Medicare will help pay for a limited skilled nursing facility stay, hospice care, or home health care, if you meet certain conditions as outlined below.

Medicare covers care in a skilled nursing home only when:

1) It is preceded by a hospital stay of at least three midnights
2) The admission occurs to a Medicare-certified nursing facility within 30 days of a prior hospital stay, and
3) The care required includes skilled nursing services and/or physical or other types of therapy.

If all three conditions are met, Medicare pays a portion of the costs for up to 100 days. For the first twenty days, Medicare pays 100 percent of the skilled nursing facility costs. For days 21-100, the patient must pay a daily co-insurance amount of up to $128/day (2008 amount). Medicare pays the balance, if any, as long as the patient continues to cooperate with therapy and shows improvement.

There is no guarantee your parent will receive 100 days of benefits. After day 100, the patient is responsible for all of the costs of a skilled nursing facility stay.

Medicare limits payments for home health care. Bills must be reasonable and necessary for part-time, or intermittent, skilled nursing care. Home health aide services are covered as well as physical therapy, occupational therapy, and speech therapy, as long as they are ordered by your parent's doctor and provided by a Medicare-certified home health agency.

Also covered are medical social services, durable medical equipment (such as wheelchairs, hospital beds, oxygen, and walkers), medical supplies, and other services. There is no co-payment for home health care. There is also no limit on the duration of services, as long as they continue to be medically necessary and the doctor requests or re-orders these services at least every 60 days.

To find out more about what Medicare does and does not pay, order the consumer handbook "Medicare & You," available at **www.Medicare.gov**. To find out what benefits your mom or dad may be eligible for, check out the Medicare Eligibility Tool on the Medicare government website, or contact Social Security at 1-800-772-1213.

Medicaid: A Safety Net For Some, But Not All

If your parents have limited income and resources, they may qualify for Medicaid. Medicaid is a joint federal and state program that helps with medical costs for people with limited means. In some states, people with Medicaid may get coverage for things like nursing home care, home care, and outpatient prescription drugs that aren't covered by Medicare as long as they meet program eligibility requirements. Between Medicare and Medicaid, your parents will have a large part of their medical costs covered.

Eligibility and covered services vary from state to state. Most often, eligibility is based on your parents' income and personal resources. But, for coverage of long term care services, your parents must also meet certain health or functional criteria in order to be eligible. If their assets and income exceed the legal limits, they may have to "spend down" in order to qualify. "Spend down" means to reduce their assets in a manner acceptable to Medicaid's rules.

If your parents are not instantly eligible for Medicaid, don't think about applying for benefits without the help of an experienced elder law attorney. Medicaid planning is definitely not a do-it-yourself project. The rules are complex and change frequently. That means the information you find on the Internet, in books and sometimes on your State's Medicaid website may be dangerously out of date.

You have no way of knowing if the information you find is accurate or not. Without reliable direction, you leave your parents and your family financially vulnerable. Expect the attorney to charge for his or her service. A good elder law attorney is worth every penny. They protect assets, help get good care for your loved one and equally as important, provide you peace of mind.

Some people believe the simple way to get below Medicaid's asset limits is to give away their assets to friends and family. As part of their determination process, each state investigates to find out if any assets were given away for the purposes of becoming eligible for Medicaid benefits. If a state finds that resources were given away, the state will assess a penalty.

The penalty can either be a delay before the onset of benefits, or it may be to stop paying for nursing home care. To avoid unnecessary penalties, talk with an experienced elder law attorney about what your parents can and can't do with their resources. To find an attorney, visit the National Academy of Elder Law attorney website at **www.NAELA.com.**

Additional information about Medicaid benefits and eligibility requirements are available at the Centers for Medicare and Medicaid Services website. **www.SurvivingEldercare.com/mcaid**

To get information on Medicaid eligibility requirements in your state, call your State Medical Assistance office. You can find their telephone number on the web at **www.SurvivingEldercare/mcare**

Help For Veterans: Hidden Program Pays Long Term Care Costs

The Department of Veterans Affairs (VA) offers three types of programs with long term care benefits.

The VA Health Care System — The first program is care from the local VA hospital. Benefits are provided to those veterans who have substantial service-related disabilities, those who receive a VA pension, or those who are considered to be low-income. Availability of services depends in part on the funds available at the veteran's medical center.

Services may include:

- Free medical exams
- Free or low cost prescription drugs
- Grants to adapt a home for a disability
- Orthotics, prosthetic devices, and hearing aids
- Home health care

State Veterans Homes — The VA has a network of State Veterans Homes offering nursing home care. Some provide assisted living services, as well. States build the facilities in partnership with the Department of Veterans affairs. Because of the rapidly aging population of veterans, demand for beds in these units is high so the homes often have waiting lists.

To locate the State Veterans Home nearest you, visit the National Association of State Veterans Homes website at **www.nasvh.org.**

Disability Income Programs — The third type of program provides disability income for veterans who have served on active duty. There are two types of disability income programs: compensation and pension.

Compensation — Compensation awards veterans an amount of money due to a disability or injury incurred while in the armed forces. While most veterans are awarded compensation when they leave the service, some veterans were exposed to incidents that did not result in noticeable disability at the time. Yet, over the years that exposure developed into a medical condition.

Examples include exposure to extreme cold, tropical disease, tuberculosis, and exposure to heavy metals. The VA does not apply an income or asset test for compensation. Benefits are received tax-free.

If your mom or dad served in the armed forces, his or her condition may be compensable by the service. To find out, check with the VA or your local County Veterans Services Association. The National Association of County Service Officers makes it easy to find your local Service Officer. Visit **www.SurvivingEldercare.com/vso**

Pension — Pension is also called "Aid and Attendance (A&A)." A&A provides supplemental monthly income to veterans who need regular help from another person with their activities of daily living. The income is available to disabled veterans and their surviving spouses who are deemed to have low income. To qualify, your parent must have been honorably discharged and must have served at least 90 days, one day of which was during a period of war.

To qualify for the pension benefit, veterans must meet certain income and asset tests. Income is adjusted for non-reimbursed medical expenses, so even veterans with otherwise higher income may qualify for assistance. The home, personal property, and automobiles are exempt from the asset test.

Visit the Department of Veterans Affairs to view available programs and services or to download a Veterans Benefits fact sheet. You can call the VA at 1-800-827-1000 to obtain information about available services in your area or call your local County Veterans Service Association. By far, the most comprehensive site on the Internet regarding the Aid and Attendance program is at **www.VeteransAid.org.**

Take Advantage of Federal and State Benefits

Millions of older people are eligible for other federal and state benefits but don't receive them because they don't know they exist. Many programs are available regardless of income or assets. A competent financial planner skilled in elder care financial planning or an Elder Law attorney can help you find those resources, figure out which benefits your parents qualify for, and help you get them.

Elderly Assistance Resources

Here are some additional resources you can tap into that specifically set aside help for the elderly:

The Social Security Administration — This federal program provides monthly income and other benefits to individuals who are at retirement age or have become disabled. Social security laws change from time to time, so check your parents' benefits at least every other year. It could mean extra income for them. **www.ssa.gov**

Medicare Rx — This federally supervised program of private insurance carriers helps pay for prescription drug costs. It requires a monthly premium payment and typically cuts the cost of drugs by about half. **www.medicare.gov**

Benefits Checkup — This site locates programs that help pay for prescription drugs, health care, utilities, and other basic needs. **www.benefitscheckup.org**

National Energy Assistance and Referral (NEAR) Project — NEAR provides information about where individuals can apply for the Low Income Home Energy Assistance Program (LIHEAP). Their toll-free phone number is 1-866-674-6327. You can send an e-mail to **energyassistance@ncat.org. www.liheap.ncat.org**

Eye Care America — This program offers eligible seniors a referral to receive a comprehensive, medical eye exam and up to one year of treatment, at no out-of-pocket cost, for any disease diagnosed during the initial exam. **www.eyecareamerica.org**

Partnership for Prescription Assistance — This program helps qualifying patients who lack prescription coverage get the medicines they need through the public or private program that is right for them. Many will get them free or nearly free. **www.pparx.org**

State Health Insurance Assistance Programs (SHIPs) are state programs that get money from the federal government to give free health insurance counseling and assistance to people with Medicare. SHIPs have counselors who might be able to answer your questions about how to pay for long term care, the coverage your parents may already have, or whether there are any government programs that may help with your health care expenses. You can find the telephone number for your SHIP at **www.Medicare.gov** or at **www.SurvivingEldercare.com** links.

Action Notes

Put what you just read to use. Jot down your ideas, thoughts, and questions as well as any actions you plan to take on the lines below. Have a question for me? E-mail me: Martin@SurvivingEldercare.com. I'm always glad to help.

"Problems arise in that one has to find a balance between what people need from you and what you need for yourself."

~ Jessye Norman

"Doing the best in this moment puts you in the best place for the next moment."

~ Oprah Winfrey

CHAPTER 12

Six Rules For Avoiding Caregiver Burnout

- What Kind Of Caregiver Are You?
- The Startling Mistake Every Family Caregiver Makes ... Including You!
- Uncommon Secrets To A Balanced Life

In Chapter 5 "Minimizing Family Conflict," you learned the importance of finding common ground with stakeholder family members and accepting the ability and willingness of other family members to help. In this chapter, I talk about finding common ground with yourself.

Families approach caregiving in one of two ways, depending on family dynamics: the entire family makes decisions as a team, or a single family member makes decisions independently.

In most families, it is the eldest daughter (or a daughter-in-law, in many cases) who shoulders the heaviest caregiving burden. Unfortunately, other family members sometimes behave as if there is only one caregiver.

I've also noticed that some caregivers assume the "Super Caregiver" role and martyr themselves as the only person who knows what mom or dad really wants. Others get so frustrated and angry with family members who do not chip in, they quit asking for help. If you see yourself in either role, or if you are an only child, and you want to provide the best possible care for your mom or dad, there are other sources of help for you.

Being the primary caregiver for an elderly or sick parent is a hard job. It gets stressful and takes a lot away from your own life. There is no way around the fact that this job is simply too hard to handle alone.

Rule #1: Know the Signs of Caregiver Stress

Most adult children overlook another very important fact: as much as you may lovingly want to provide the care your parents need, doing so can make you sick.

Literally.

When you care for a loved one, stress comes with the territory. What you might not know is that 25 percent of caregivers report their health suffers in some way as a result of their caregiving role.

Studies have proven over and over again that stress negatively affects the immune system. It increases the time it takes for wounds to heal and the time it takes to rebound from cold and flu viruses. According to some studies, between 75 and 90 percent of primary care doctor visits are for stress-related difficulties.

> ***ELDER FACTS***
> *Extreme stress can take as much as ten years off of a family caregiver's life. Source: Peter S. Arno: Economic Value of Informal Caregiving (2006)*

The pressures and multiple responsibilities of being a family caregiver produce what researchers call a "caregiver burden." This refers to the multiple whammies you get from the physical, psychological, emotional, social, and financial demands of providing care to aging parents.

Researchers have directly linked caregiver burden with higher levels of stress that weaken the immune system. When your immune system is compromised, you are more likely to become ill yourself.

Researchers point to stress as a contributing or aggravating cause to a long list of various medical conditions, including:

Chronic pain	Diabetes	Infertility
Migraines	Asthma	Rheumatoid arthritis
Ulcers	Heart disease	Irritable bowel syndrome
Heartburn	PMS	Skin problems
High blood pressure	Obesity	Chronic fatigue syndrome

The American Institute of Stress has also linked stress to all leading causes of death: heart disease, cancer, lung ailments, accidents, cirrhosis of the liver, and suicide.

ELDER FACTS

Counseling and support groups, used along with respite and other services, have positive direct effects on the health of caregivers and help them continue their caregiving role with less stress and greater satisfaction. Source: The Stress Process Among Dementia Spouse Caregivers: Are Caregivers at Risk for Negative Health Behavior Change? (Research on Aging 20[3])

It is seriously important for you to learn how to handle the stress that accompanies your decision to become a caregiver.

When you get sick you can't be there to provide the care your loved one needs. Generally when the primary caregiver gets ill, the person needing the care ends up in the one place no one wants: a nursing home or an assisted living facility.

Rule #2: Find and Accept Help

Most caregivers fail to look for help initially for three reasons:

- They are too busy dealing with the immediacy and newness of the situation.
- They have a sense they have to do it themselves.
- They don't know that resources exist to help them.

Dr. Marion Somers, author of "Elder Care Made Easier," and a leading expert on caregiving, refers to this problem as "reinventing the wheel." While speaking with her just before she appeared on my "Ask Mr. Eldercare" radio show, she mentioned that most families dealing with elder care have no idea how to care for a loved one.

This is not a blanket condemnation of anyone's heart or intention. It is a simple recognition of how new and confusing eldercare is for all of us, and how difficult it can be to find the necessary help.

The issue of providing care to long-lived elders is a brand new societal phenomenon. Never in the history of the world has a generation found themselves caring for their parents as long as we will. It is a case of the biblical societal imperative of "honor thy father and mother" clashing with modern society's improved longevity, delayed child birth, and scattered families.

Because the elder care problem is new, we have no paradigm established and no road map through this new societal landscape. You are reading this book, in part, because you are looking for that road map and those resources to make your life better.

The good news is you DO have resources available outside your family to help relieve the caregiver burden. While the network is vast, the bad news is that it is generally hidden from our normal daily activities. You need to know where to look to find it.

In Chapter 4, "Find The Right Help Fast," you will find the best entry points into this wonderful pool of help.

I have also included a huge list of support organizations in the back of this book. A simple phone call can tap you into important resources right in your home town.

Rule #3: Learn to Set Limits

It is one thing to know about available help. Using it is another matter.

Caregivers can understandably have a difficult time setting limits on the time, energy, and attention they dedicate to taking care of a parent. When you have been emotionally attached to a person for four, five, or six decades, you can't be distant about their well-being. Yet, it is distance and perspective that you need in order to minimize the stress.

So how do you do that? Is it possible to step back from the emotion of the situation and gain positive perspective?

The answer is a surprising "yes," but not for everyone.

Kathleen Divita is a Houston psychotherapist, providing care for her aging father. She admits the two of them "did not have the friendliest relationship over the years." She cares about him, though, and has been providing care to him for a number of years.

She told me, "When the caregiver role first lands in your lap, it takes on a life of its own. You are driven to get things organized, to take care of people, and settle everything down. At that point, you are in it. There's really not much distance."

"Over time," she continued, "it becomes clear that after you've run into some issues, you need to rethink how you can handle the relationship. It's very hard to do depending on your past history. If you've been a good limit setter in the past and you have been good about setting boundaries, if you were okay with saying 'no' and if you're not run through with a whole lot of guilt, it's easier to do."

"If you're one of those people who has all those things going on, it's much harder to gain a more objective perspective."

ELDER FACTS

Recipe To Avoid Caregiver Burnout: Make time for yourself. Get adequate sleep, proper nutrition and exercise regularly. Socialize with friends. Make time for family and to be alone. Ask for and accept help.

Rule #4: Manage Your Time

Trying to do everything yourself is the leading cause of caregiver burnout. Your biggest problem as a caregiver is that you might try to assume the entire burden on your own.

You need to decide what you are able and willing to do and stick to it. Without help, you put your own health at risk.

You need to find out what help is available and how to get it. (See Chapter 4, "Find The Right Help Fast.") It's the only way you will be able to effectively manage the various aspects of caregiving.

The secret to maintaining balance is to know how to manage your time and getting your family to understand what you are going through.

Another key to maintaining your emotional balance is scheduling time for yourself.

It's hard to fit the emotional, physical, and financial demands of aging parents into an already busy life. A common mistake most caregivers make is to believe they must choose between their needs, the needs of their family, and the needs of their parents.

As the demands of caregiving increase, you will naturally have less free time for yourself and your family. Remember: how much time you spend providing direct care is ultimately your decision. Make an agreement with yourself to always budget time for you.

A common difficulty caregivers face is a spouse or child who feels neglected when the caregiver spends time caring for their parents. Make it a point to schedule special "dates" with both. Whatever it is you and your spouse enjoy doing most, schedule it. Set aside special time to be with each child.

You can use modern technology to stay connected with your children, too. I've heard of a caregiver who, unable to attend her daughter's volleyball game, asked a good friend to video the game. That way she was able to sit with her daughter and relive the game after she had handled her mom's needs.

You may need to guard what spare time you have. The more intense the caregiving oversight becomes, the greater your need will be for time control and calling upon the help of others. Set contact rules for family members and friends. Answering their questions one at a time about your parent's health can wipe out your spare time and drain your energy.

The Internet provides several excellent communication vehicles that allow you to keep interested family and friends up to date with your loved one's situation.

One option is setting up a blog.

A blog is an online journal where you can post updates as often as you like. Blogs allow you to post text, photos, and videos allowing family and friends to keep up with the latest news you want to share. Unless the blog platform you select has privacy controls allowing you to determine who can see your posts, everyone in the world can see what is posted on a blog. The best hosting platform I have found for posting journals with privacy options is at www.livejournal.com. If you use a platform without privacy controls, be selective with the information you post online.

You can set up free blogs at the following sites:

www.blogger.com
www.wordpress.com
www.livejournal.com
www.thoughts.com
www.blogs.com

A more private solution is to set up a Yahoo group. It's a snap to do and allows friends and family members to communicate quickly and easily.

A Yahoo Group is a "chat service." You can set up your account as a private group and limit who can join. Messages between participants are only seen by those you approve. It's a real money saver, too, if you have family members spread across the country (or the world, for that matter). Chat histories are stored on Yahoo's computers so there is some chance a hacker could see your chat histories. Although the likelihood is small, you will want to factor it into your decision.

Another solution that makes communication fast and simple is called Skype (**www.Skype.com**). A simple, free download allows you to talk to anyone else with a Skype account, anywhere in the world for free, using VOIP technology (voice over internet protocol). All you need is your computer, an Internet connection, and a microphone.

Skype has a nifty chat system, too. It allows you to archive your chats and store them on your computer. You can invite your whole family to a meeting and exchange information and concerns in real time. Skype offers a paid service, too, that allows you to call any landline phone in the country for as little as $3 per month.

Unlike Yahoo Groups, chat histories are not stored anywhere on the Skype network. In other words, no one else on Skype will ever be able to see any of your chat histories except you and the person with whom you are chatting. Chats are a handy way to easily keep track of your conversations about your loved ones online.

If events are changing rapidly, having a blog or a Skype or Yahoo account enables you to keep everyone updated from anywhere you have an Internet connection.

A low-tech solution, when the situation warrants, is setting up a phone tree. You have a prearranged agreement with several friends and family members to pass along information to several others.

Rule #5: Build and Use Your Support System

As a caregiver, you tend to put your needs after those of your parent. While caregiving has its many rewards, burnout is not one of them. If you sense increased feelings of isolation, stress, guilt, depression, helplessness, anger, or resentment, it's time to back away from caregiving and give yourself some space.

This is where your support system comes to the rescue. Use it.

Some caregivers reach a point where they feel unable to give any more. If that happens to you, consider hiring help or moving your parent into a community residential environment. If things feel desperate, you may want to speak with a counselor.

Don't wait to seek support until you are already overwhelmed. View your situation realistically. Realize you can only do so much and be patient with yourself.

Your whole life isn't caregiving.

Although you choose to be there because of your love and sense of duty, you have a right to good health and a right to love yourself.

Left unhandled, caregiver stress can lead to "caregiver burnout."

Burnout is a total loss of motivation. It occurs most often when a person's devotion to a cause or relationship does not produce the desired results. If you are providing care to a loved one, and you have lost your incentive to push on, you may be suffering from it.

Burnout is common with family caregivers. It is a less severe form of depression, anxiety, and mood disorder. Some of the symptoms include physical and emotional exhaustion, frequent illnesses, withdrawal from personal relationships, and increased absences from work.

It's all directly connected to caregiver stress.

The constant stress of caregiving can take its toll. It can drain your energy and make you feel tired all the time. Mustering the power to get out of bed can be hard because you have lost your former level of physical strength.

If you are not the "ground zero" caregiver, stay alert to the signs of caregiver burnout in the person who is. One of the most loving steps you can take when you see someone working themselves sick as a caregiver is to steer that person toward help. If you are that caregiver, keep these questions handy and use them as a simple self check for emotional exhaustion.

- Do you find yourself more moody and subject to wild mood swings?
- Do you feel sad at times without reason?
- Do you find yourself impatient and easily frustrated?
- Do you resist having others close by?
- Have you stopped seeking fun relationships with friends and family?
- Are you more pessimistic about life?
- Have otherwise small matters become weighty?

A positive answer to just one of these questions means you may be suffering from caregiver burnout. If so, it's time to make other arrangements to care for your loved one.

Rule #6: Get a Coach

If you find you cannot gain an objective perspective, think about hiring a professional "life coach" to guide you through your new caregiving territory.

A life coach can be a psychotherapist experienced in elder care issues like Kathleen, a geriatric care manager, or one of the new breed of life coaches who focuses on bringing balance to the work, life, and family.

You are looking for someone who "knows the territory" — someone who has the knowledge, skill base, and training to help you navigate through the elder care terrain. Finding a professional with the right skills can help you operate better in this strange new world in which you find yourself.

Anybody who has been "up the mountain" a couple of times can help you walk that path and do it safely. I don't consider myself to be a psychotherapist, but because I have experienced so much of this through my clients and my own family issues, I have spent a lot of time walking up and down the mountain path and learning how to handle the storms and surprises along the trail.

The problem is that finding people like Kathleen and me is not that simple.

To find out what you need, you must first connect with the elder care community. Once you open that door, you will be amazed how much support is available.

Disease-specific support groups are a good place to start. These organizations have a lot of connections you can plug yourself into. You will also meet the "old salts" who have been caring for a loved one with the same issues as your mom or dad for four, five, or even ten years. You will gain a lot from their insight.

The fastest way to find a support group is to simply go to the Internet and type in whatever particular disease issue you are dealing with, followed by "support group" (with the quotation marks). For example, searching for a cancer support group would look like this: cancer "support group." If you don't have access to a computer (or someone who does), refer to the huge list of resources in the back of this book.

If you will be hiring a geriatric care manager, psychotherapist, or life coach, these questions will help you decide if someone is the right coach for you:

- How many years have you been practicing?
- What is your experience with caregiving issues?
- What is your experience with the elderly?
- Have you ever been a caregiver yourself or have you dealt with it in your family?

- Have you ever worked with (name of disease) issues before?

Some coaches will provide an overall course of action and send you on your way asking you to call again if you get stuck. Others prefer a series of meetings to make sure you get a solid foundation from which to operate. You have to decide what approach works best for you.

If you like the person, if you feel comfortable with him or her, and if you sense some compatibility, consider hiring that person. Try them out for a session or two. If it works, continue. If not, let the person know you are not comfortable and ask them to refer you to someone else. Most are happy to do so.

Fees will vary depending on where you are located, the type of help required, and the experience level of the professional. In Houston, you can expect to pay $100-$275 per hour. There can be an initial assessment fee, too, so be sure to ask about that.

If your financial circumstances limit your ability to pay fees, ask the person you are considering if he or she will work with you at a lower hourly cost. Some will. If not, check with some of the United Way agencies in your area. Often, they make services available on a sliding scale based on income and assets.

Some professionals commit themselves to certain groups, such as cancer survivors or families dealing with Alzheimer's disease and dementia. Generally, the more experience an individual has with a particular disease group the more helpful he or she can be.

Good coaches can be worth their weight in gold because they know the landscape. They know the resources that will help you best and can plug you into them quickly.

Therapeutic Meltdowns

Taking over someone else's life can become an overpowering experience. Realizing that the well-being of the person who raised you is now completely in your hands can issue a sobering jolt of a new reality.

It is a weighty realization that often changes your perspective on life and the sense of responsibility you have toward others. When the pressure balloons up inside more than you believe you can bear, a therapeutic meltdown might be in order.

What is a therapeutic meltdown?

It occurs during those times when you feel so helpless, overwhelmed, and tired that you put your face in your hands and have a good, sobbing cry. It is a great way of releasing in times of stress. It is perfectly normal.

It seems to happen when you realize you are making yet another decision you never thought you would have to make for someone else. You don't know if it is the decision they would make if they could.

If your parents could participate in the decision, it would make life so much easier for all of you, but when your mom or dad is no longer able to make those decisions, it sets up a terrible internal conflict.

Maybe it's the time you have to take the car keys and the car away from your dad. It could be when you actually sell it and watch a stranger drive off in your dad's car. Maybe it's the first day you leave your mom behind in an assisted living community and walk out the door.

It can be as simple as the time you take your dad to the drugstore to buy razor blades for his shaver. You see he is disoriented in the store. He gets lost. He is weak and can barely make his way down the aisles.

When he checks out he hands the cashier his credit card. Because he has recently moved to your city, he is not in the store's computer system. The cashier asks, "What is your phone number?" He doesn't know it. "What is your address?" He doesn't know that either.

In the past, he would pull out his platinum card and watch people quickly respond. Now he can't answer simple questions about his phone number and address.

He's lost. You know it. You realize you can't stop the decline. It hurts. The stress balloons inside.

And you melt down.

There is nothing wrong with a good cry now and then. If these "meltdowns" happen too often, though, they lose their therapeutic value. If you find yourself in that situation, it is time to get yourself some help. You could be headed toward caregiver burnout.

It is understandable for you to feel angry, frightened, insecure, and unsafe on a societal level.

It is better if a family member can be there for you as back-up, but sometimes that's not practical or possible. Another option is using respite care offered by Adult Day Care Centers or personal service agencies in your community.

Kathleen also passed on this tip:

"There is no one-size-fits-all easy rule to follow. Don't simply react in a knee-jerk fashion. Don't go with your impulses. They usually get you in trouble. If your mom or dad is upset or angry or really distressed, the best thing to do is just to be with them. There is no need to do anything. Just be there for them."

It is also important to acknowledge your feelings if your caregiving journey starts feeling like an emotional roller coaster. Feeling guilt, frustration, or resentment is natural when your parents' demands consume you.

Action Notes

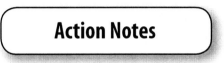

Put what you just read to use. Jot down your ideas, thoughts, and questions as well as any actions you plan to take on the lines below. Have a question for me? E-mail me: Martin@SurvivingEldercare.com. I'm always glad to help.

"Let us not look back in anger or forward in fear, but around in awareness."

~ James Thurber

"Everything can be taken from a man but the last of human freedoms, the right to choose one's attitude in any given set of circumstances — the right to choose one's own way."

~ Victor Frankl

CHAPTER 13

Moving Forward With Confidence

- Two Top Antidotes To Anxiety, Frustration, Fear and Worry
- Stop Beating Yourself Up!
- Remove Your Rear View Mirror

Supervising the care of an aging parent will change your life. The experience will lead you down a number of different paths and it will help you learn more about yourself than you can probably imagine.

With the task comes a number of unanticipated challenges — important issues you never thought about in the past. Health care, housing, legal matters, personal safety, financial concerns, and family issues will begin to take center stage in your life.

As with any new job, elder care has a learning curve. Use what you learn every day to build on tomorrow.

If you find yourself upset, fearful, confused, frustrated, worried, and stressed, I understand. This is not necessarily an easy road to walk. The two most powerful antidotes to fear, worry, and stress are education and action.

Start by understanding your mom or dad's wants. If they are unknown, or if your loved one is not able to express them, cobble together a family consensus.

Accept your family's limitations, as well. Years ago, one of my clients taught me it is emotionally unsafe to use a comparative yardstick to measure the contributions of another family member against yours. She found herself feeling "used" by her brother. She constantly whined about his lack of involvement. One morning she realized she had allowed herself to become a victim of his decisions rather than the leader of her mom's care.

At that point, she decided she would be more assertive in requesting help. She did not get mad. She didn't whine. She took control. When she needed help, she simply stated the situation and put the responsibility on his shoulders. She was startled by how easily he accepted and stepped in to help.

The lesson? Be proactive, be direct, and expect others to respond well. They often do.

Does it always work? Of course not. But, if you don't ask for help, you will never hear anyone say "Yes." When you do ask, you may be surprised by the positive response you get.

Realize, too, it is okay if you are not the one providing the care directly. Not everyone is hard-wired to be a hands-on caregiver. Find your strengths and use them to your mom or dad's benefit. Call on family, friends, health associations, social support groups, and professionals to find help with the tasks you are unwilling, or unable, to do.

Because caregiving can be outrageously expensive, find and use every benefit available to your parent. Financial assistance is available on the federal level through Social Security, Medicare, and Veteran's benefits, on the state level with Medicaid, and on the city level with health clinics and senior centers. On the local level, be sure to check with local churches or synagogues and with local United Way agencies.

Throughout this book, in the Resource Section, and on my website, I give you hundreds of organizations that are ready and willing to lend a hand. Where available, I have provided each organization's phone number, mailing address, website, and e-mail address.

It will take some effort to line up assistance from these various resources, but the contacts, information, and support they provide can save you time, effort, stress, and money. The only way to do it is to roll up your shirt sleeves and start calling.

It is easy to forget about your needs when a parent requires help to remain safe and maintain dignity. There is a huge risk of losing yourself in the caregiving process — to subordinate your needs to those of your ailing parent.

If there is one piece of wisdom you take from everything I have said, let it be this:

Take care of yourself.

Self-sacrifice does not have to be part of the solution. If your dedication makes you sick or causes you to burn out, who will be there for your parents and for your family? To maintain your emotional, physical, and mental strength, it is important to realize and accept your limitations. We all have them. Be honest with yourself. Lean on your strengths and be willing to admit when you need a break.

It is possible the results of a decision will turn out to be something other than what you wanted. Accept it and move on. The best you can do is the best you can do. Beating yourself up over it — or letting others do so — serves no purpose.

The stories of two families make this point vividly clear:

One of my clients decided it would be best to move her mother to an assisted living facility. While in that community, her mom fell and broke a hip. During the operation to mend the hip, her mom's heart stopped, causing irreparable brain damage. The damage was severe enough to require nursing home care for her mom.

The daughter agonizes over her decision to use an assisted living facility. Maybe, she thinks, it would have been better to let her mom remain in her home and hire aides to be with her. Was her decision a good one?

Another family decided to keep their dad at home with aides rather than move him into an assisted living community. In the morning, he enjoyed sitting on his front porch, drinking his coffee, and looking at the flowers surrounding the deck. One morning, the aide hired to assist him walked into the kitchen to warm up his coffee. She had done so many times over the prior three months. The dad decided to walk down the steps to look at his roses, as he frequently did.

This time he slipped.

He hit his head on one of the steps and was rushed to the hospital. During his procedure, his heart also stopped, resulting in brain damage that now requires 24-hour nursing home care. This family struggles with their decision to keep their dad at home. Would it have been better to move him to an assisted living facility?

Each family reached the same fork in the road, but each chose a different path. They both made the best decision possible at the time, yet each one now second-guesses that decision.

There is no way to tell if taking another path would have had better results. Second-guessing yourself only adds to an already heavy emotional burden.

Providing care to your mother or father requires you to get your arms around a lot of information and to become a good manager of time and resources. It is my sincere prayer that the information shared inside this book, and its companion website, will make life easier for you.

At the beginning of this book, I offered to help should you find yourself needing help with a caregiver situation. The offer is sincere. Feel free to add me to your support system.

Send me an e-mail at **Martin@SurvivingEldercare.com** and let me know what help you need. I look forward to hearing from you.

If you have not done so already, take the time right now to visit **www.SurvivingEldercare.com/buyer**. You will find a lot of additional helpful ideas and resources waiting for you when you get there.

Action Notes

Put what you just read to use. Jot down your ideas, thoughts, and questions as well as any actions you plan to take on the lines below. Have a question for me? E-mail me: Martin@SurvivingEldercare.com. I'm always glad to help.

RESOURCE DIRECTORY

Alphabetical Listing of Resources

AAA Foundation for Traffic Safety
607 14th Street, NW, Suite 201
Washington, DC 20005
Phone: (202) 638-5944, Fax: (202) 638-5943
Web site: http://www.aaafts.org

AARP
Fulfillment
601 E Street, NW
Washington, DC 20049
Phone: (888) 687-2277 or (800) 424-3410
Web site: http://www.aarp.org

AARP Grandparent Information Center
601 E Street, NW
Washington, DC 20049
Phone: (888) 687-2277 or (800) 424-3410
Web site: http://www.aarp.org/families/grandparents

ABA Commission on Law and Aging
740 15th Street, NW
Washington, DC 20005
Phone: (202) 662-8690
Web site: http://www.abanet.org/aging

Abilities!
201 I.U. Willets Road
Albertson, NY 11507
Phone: (516) 465-1400 or (516) 747-5400
Web site: http://www.ncds.org

ABLEDATA
(An assistive technology information exchange, serving the nation's disability, rehabilitation, and senior communities)
8630 Fenton Street, Suite 930
Silver Spring, MD 20910
Phone: (800) 227-0216 or (301) 608-8998, Fax: (301) 608-8958, TDD: (301) 608-8912
Web site: http://www.abledata.com

Access America for Seniors
Web site: **http://www.seniors.gov**

Administración del Envejeciente (Hispanic Aging Resources)
Administration on Aging
One Massachusetts Avenue, Suites 4100/5100
Washington, DC 20201
Phone: (202) 619-0724, Fax: (202) 357-3555
Web site: http://www.aoa.gov/language/language_espanol.asp

Administration on Aging
One Massachusetts Avenue, Suites 4100/5100
Washington, DC 20201
Phone: (202) 619-0724, Fax: (202) 357-3555
Web site: http://www.aoa.dhhs.gov

Aging with Dignity
(Emphasizes improving care for the elderly at the end of their lives)
P.O. Box 1661
820 E. Park Avenue, Suite D100
Tallahassee, FL 32301
Phone: (888) 594-7437 or (850) 681-2010, Fax: (850) 681-2481
Web site: http://www.agingwithdignity.org

AirMed International
1000 Urban Center Drive, Suite 470
Birmingham, AL 35242
Phone: (800) 356-2161 or (205) 443-4840, Fax: (205) 443-4841
Web site: http://www.airmed.com

ALS Association
(The only national not-for-profit health organization dedicated solely to the fight against ALS. Its mission is to find a cure for and improve living with Amyotrophic Lateral Sclerosis.)
27001 Agoura Road, Suite 150
Calabasas Hills, CA 91301
Phone: (818) 880-9007
Web site: http://www.alsa.org

Alzheimer's Association
(Provides latest information and research on the disease)
225 North Michigan Avenue, 17th Floor
Chicago, IL 60601
Phone: (800) 272-3900 or (312) 335-8700, Fax: (866) 699-1246, TDD: (866) 403-3073
Web site: http://www.alz.org

Alzheimer's Disease Education & Referral Center
ADEAR Center
P.O. Box 8250
Silver Spring, MD 20907
Phone: (800) 438-4380, Fax: (301) 495-3334
Web site: http://www.alzheimers.org

American Academy of Facial Plastic and Reconstructive Surgery
310 S. Henry Street
Alexandria, VA 22314
Phone: (703) 299-9291, Fax: (703) 299-8898
Web site: http://www.aafprs.org

American Association for Geriatric Psychiatry
7910 Woodmont Avenue, Suite 1050
Bethesda, MD 20814
Phone: (301) 654-7850, Fax: (301) 654-4137
Web site: http://www.aagpgpa.org

American Association of Daily Money Managers
(Assists people who have difficulty managing their personal monetary affairs such as paying bills, balancing checkbooks, preparing and delivering bank deposits, credit negotiations, general organizational activities, etc.)
174 Crestview Drive
Bellefonte, PA 16823
Phone: (877) 326-5991, Fax: (814) 355-2452
Web site: http://www.aadmm.com

American Association of Homes and Services for the Aging (AAHSA)
2519 Connecticut Avenue, NW
Washington, DC 20008
Phone: (202) 783-2242, Fax: (202) 783-2255
Web site: http://www.aahsa.org

American Bar Association
321 N. Clark Street
Chicago, IL 60611
Phone: (800) 285-2221
Web site: http://www.abanet.org

American Board of Medical Specialties
(To find out if a doctor is board certified)
1007 Church Street, Suite 404
Evanston, IL 60201
Phone: (866) 275-2267 or (847) 491-9091
Web site: http://www.abms.org

American Brain Tumor Association
2720 River Road
Des Plaines, IL 60018
Phone: (847) 827-9910, Fax: (847) 827-9918
Web site: http://www.abta.org

American Council of the Blind
1155 15th Street, NW, Suite 1004
Washington, DC 20005
Phone: (800) 424-8666 or (202) 467-5081, Fax: (202) 467-5085
Web site: http://www.acb.org

American Diabetes Association
(Provides access to new research and educational materials)
1701 N. Beauregard Street
Alexandria, VA 22311
Phone: (800) 342-2383
Web site: http://www.diabetes.org

American Dietetic Association
(Nutrition information for older Americans)
120 S. Riverside Plaza, Suite 2000
Chicago, IL 60606
Phone: (800) 877-1600
Web site: http://www.eatright.org

American Federation for Aging Research (AFAR)
(Funds scientific research on aging)
55 West 39th Street, 16th Floor
New York, NY 10018
Phone: (212) 703-9977, Fax: (212) 997-0330
Web site: http://www.infoaging.org

American Geriatrics Society
Empire State Building
350 Fifth Avenue, Suite 801
New York, NY 10118
Phone: (212) 308-1414, Fax: (212) 832-8646
Web site: http://www.americangeriatrics.org

American Health Assistance Foundation (AHAF)
(Alzheimer's Family Relief Program)
22512 Gateway Center Drive
Clarksburg, MD 20871
Phone: (800) 437-2423 or (301) 948-3244, Fax: (301) 258-9454
Web site: http://www.ahaf.org

American Health Care Association (AHCA)
1201 L Street, NW
Washington, DC 20005
Phone: (202) 842-4444, Fax: (202) 842-3860
Web site: http://www.ahcancal.org

American Hearing Research Foundation
8 South Michigan Avenue, Suite 814
Chicago, CA 60603
Phone: (312) 726-9670, Fax: (312) 726-9695
Web site: http://www.american-hearing.org

American Heart Association
7272 Greenville Avenue
Dallas, TX 75231
Phone: (800) 242-8721
Web site: http://www.americanheart.org

American Hospice Foundation
(Provides helpful information on hospice care)
2120 L Street, NW, Suite 200
Washington, DC 20037
Phone: (800) 347-1413 or (202) 223-0204, Fax: (202) 223-0208
Web site: http://www.americanhospice.org

American Institute of Certified Public Accountants (AICPA)
1211 Avenue of the Americas
New York, NY 10036
Phone: (888) 777-7077 or (212) 596-6200
Web site: http://www.aicpa.org

American Liver Foundation
75 Maiden Lane, Suite 603
New York, NY 10038
Phone: (212) 668-1000, Fax: (212) 483-8179
Web site: http://www.liverfoundation.org

American Lung Association
(Find a local chapter or search the site for information on all lung topics)
61 Broadway, 6th Floor
New York, NY 10006
Phone: (800) 586-4872 or (212) 315-8700
Web site: http://www.lungusa.org

American Medical Association
(Online doctor finder and health information)
515 State Street
Chicago, IL 60610
Phone: (800) 621-8335
Web site: http://www.ama-assn.org

American Parkinson Disease Association
135 Parkinson Avenue
Staten Island, NY 10305
Phone: (800) 223-2732 or (718) 981-8001,
Fax: (718) 981-4399
Web site: http://www.apdaparkinson.org

American Red Cross
2025 E Street, NW
Washington, DC 20006
Phone: (800) 733-2767
Web site: http://www.redcross.org

American Society on Aging (ASA)
(Provides information, education, training, and other resources regarding all aspects of aging)
833 Market Street, #511
San Francisco, CA 94103
Phone: (800) 537-9728 or (415) 974-9600, Fax: (415) 974-0300
Web site: http://www.asaging.org

American Speech-Language-Hearing Association
2200 Research Boulevard
Rockville, MD 20850
Phone: (800) 638-8255, Fax: (301) 296-8580, TDD: (301) 296-5650
Web site: http://www.asha.org

American Stroke Association
(Solely focused on reducing disability and death from stroke)
National Center
7272 Greenville Avenue
Dallas, TX 75231
Phone: (888) 478-7653
Web site: http://www.strokeassociation.org

American Trauma Society
7611 South Osborne Road, Suite 202
Upper Marlboro, MD 20772
Phone: (800) 556-7890 or (301) 574-4300, Fax: (301) 574-4301
Web site: http://www.amtrauma.org

Americans for Better Care of the Dying (ABCD)
1700 Diagonal Road, Suite 635
Alexandria, VA 22314
Phone: (703) 647-8505, Fax: (703) 837-1233
Web site: http://www.abcd-caring.org

Arthritis Foundation
(Provides support for over one hundred types of arthritis and related conditions)
P.O. Box 7669
Atlanta, GA 30357
Phone: (800) 283-7800
Web site: http://www.arthritis.org

Assisted Living Federation of America
1650 King Street, Suite 602
Alexandria, VA 22314
Phone: (703) 894-1805, Fax: (703) 894-1831
Web site: http://www.alfa.org

Association for Protection of the Elderly (APE)
728A West Main Street
Lexington, SC 29072
Phone: (800) 569-7345, Fax: (803) 356-6212
Web site: http://www.elder-abuse-foundation.com

Benefits Checkup
(Database of federal and state assistance programs for the elderly)
Web site: http://www.benefitscheckup.org

Benefits Link, Inc.
1298 Minnesota Avenue, Suite H
Winter Park, FL 32789
Phone: (407) 644-4146, Fax: (407) 644-2151
Web site: http://www.benefitslink.com

BR Anchor Relocation Experts
4596 Capital Dome Drive
Jacksonville, FL 32246
Phone: (800) 735-9209, Fax: (904) 641-1136
Web site: http://www.branchor.com

Brain Injury Association of America
1608 Spring Hill Road, Suite 110
Vienna, VA 22182
Phone: (703) 761-0750, Fax: (703) 761-0755
Web site: http://www.biausa.org

Brookdale Center for Healthy Aging and Longevity of Hunter College
425 E. 25th Street, 13th Floor North
New York, NY 10010
Phone: (212) 481-3780, Fax: (212) 481-3791
Web site: http://www.brookdale.org

Cancer Care
(A national non-profit organization. Provides free professional help to people with all cancers through counseling, education, information and referral and direct financial assistance.)
275 Seventh Avenue, 22nd Floor
New York, NY 10001
Phone: (800) 813-4673, Fax: (212) 712-8495
Web site: http://www.cancercare.org

Caregiver.com
(A leading provider of information, support, and guidance for family and professional caregivers)
Phone: (800) 829-2734
Web site: http://www.caregiver.org

CaregiverProducts.com
(Products that make caregiving easier and life better for those with physical need: diability aids, elderly care products, handicap aids, geriatric aids, home medical supplies, nursing home supplies, and assistive devices.)
Attention: Amy Wright, PT
135 Floyd G. Harrell Drive
Grenada, MS 38901
Phone: (662) 294-1444, Fax: (662) 294-1445
Web site: http://www.Eldercare1.com/wri

Caregiving.com
(Offers access to support, information and resources you need when you care for an aging relative)
P.O. Box 224
Park Ridge, IL 60068
Phone: (773) 343-6341
Web site: **http://www.caregiving.com**

Center for Medicare Advocacy
(Focuses on health care rights, especially the needs of Medicare beneficiaries)
National Office
P.O. Box 350
Willimantic, CT 06226
Phone: (860) 456-7790, Fax: (860) 456-2614
Web site: http://www.medicareadvocacy.org

Center for Work and the Family
7 Santa Maria Way
Orinda, CA 94563
Phone: (925) 258-5400, Fax: (925) 376-3766
Web site: http://www.centerforworkandfamily.com

Center Watch Clinical Trials Listing Service
(Offers information related to clinical trials and new drug therapies)
22 Thompson Place, 47FI
Boston, MA 02210
Phone: (617) 856-5900, Fax: (617) 856-5901
Web site: http://www.centerwatch.com

Centers for Medicare and Medicaid Services
(Provides information on all facets of Medicaid)
7500 Security Boulevard
Baltimore, MD 21244
Phone: (800) 633-4227, TDD: (877) 486-2048
Web site: http://www.cms.hhs.gov

Certified Financial Planner Board of Standards
1700 Broadway, Suite 2100
Denver, CO 80290
Phone: (888) 237-6275 or (303) 830-7500, Fax: (303) 860-7388
Web site: http://www.cfp.net

Children of Aging Parents (CAPS)
(Assists elder-caregivers with information, referrals, and support)
P.O. Box 167
Richboro, PA 18954
Phone: (800) 227-7294
Web site: http://www.caps4caregivers.org

Choice in Dying
(State-specific living wills and advance directives)
1035 30th Street, NW
Washington, DC 20007
Phone: (202) 338-9790, Fax: (202) 338-0242

Christopher Reeve Paralysis Foundation
636 Morris Turnpike, Suite 3A
Short Hills, NJ 07078
Phone: (800) 225-0292
Web site: http://www.christopherreeve.org

Coalition for Quality Patient Care
1275 K Street, NW, Suite 602
Washington, DC 20005
Phone: (202) 789-3606

Commission on Accreditation of Rehabilitation Facilities (CARF)
1730 Rhode Island Avenue, NW, Suite 209
Washington, DC 20036
Phone: (202) 587-5001, Fax: (202) 587-5009
Web site: http://www.carf.org

Community Transportation Association of America
1341 G Street, NW, 10th Floor
Washington, DC 20005
Phone: (202) 628-1480, Fax: (202) 737-9197
Web site: http://www.ctaa.org

Consumer Information Center
(To obtain hundreds of federal consumer publications)
Department WWW
Pueblo, CO 81009
Phone: (888) 878-3256
Web site: http://www.pueblo.gsa.gov

Council of Better Business Bureaus
(To locate local offices in United States and Canada)
4200 Wilson Boulevard, Suite 800
Arlington, VA 22203
Phone: (703) 276-0100, Fax: (703) 525-8277
Web site: **http://www.bbb.org**

Dementia.com
(Provides information for caregivers and healthcare professionals. Subscribers can customize the site, receive newsletters and access Medline mail service, providing access to over three million online articles. Primarily intended for European audiences but chock full of great information about dementia and Alzheimer's Disease.)
Web site: http://www.dementia.com

Department of Veterans Affairs
1722 I Street, NW
Washington, DC 20421
Phone: (800) 827-1000, TDD: (800) 829-4833
Web site: http://www.va.gov

Diabetes.com
(An informative site sponsored by GlaxoSmithKline Pharmaceuticals. Provides diabetes facts, health tips and guidance for caregivers.)
Web site: http://www.diabetes.com

Direct Marketing Association
(To be removed from unsolicited mailing lists)
Attention: Mail Preference Service
P.O. Box 9008
Farmingdale, NY 11735
Web site: http://www.dmachoice.org/mps/mps_consumer_description.php

Disability Resources
Web site: http://www.disabilityresources.org

Disabled and Alone
61 Broadway, Suite 510
New York, NY 10006
Phone: (800) 995-0066 or (212) 532-6740, Fax: (212) 532-3588
Web site: http://www.disabledandalone.org

Doctor's Guide
(A personalized Internet resource of medical news and information on everything from Alzheimer's to viral infections.)
Web site: http://www.docguide.com

Dr. Koop
(Provides information on health and fitness)
225 Arizona Avenue, #256
Santa Monica, CA 90401
Phone: (310) 395-5700
Web site: http://www.drkoop.com

Drug Pill Identifier
(Basic drug safety means you should never take a pill if you are not 100% sure what it is you are taking. Uses a handy drug-picture database to help you easily identify an unlabeled drug in a cabinet or pill case.)
Web site: http://www.drugs.com/pill_identification.html

Easter Seals
230 West Monroe Street, Suite 1800
Chicago, IL 60606
Phone: (800) 221-6827 or (312) 726-6200, Fax: (312) 726-1494, TDD: (312) 726-4258
Web site: http://www.easterseals.com

Eden Alternative
(Improving the quality of life for people who live in long-term care facilities)
111 Blue Oak Lane
Wimberley, TX 78676
Phone: (512) 847-6061, Fax: (512) 847-6191
Web site: http://www.edenalt.com

Elder Law Answers
P.O. Box 29
260 West Exchange Street, Suite 004
Providence, RI 02903
Phone: (866) 267-0947
Web site: http://www.elderlawanswers.com

Eldercare Locator
(Helps older adults and their caregivers find services for seniors)
Phone: (800) 677-1116
Web site: http://www.eldercare.gov

ElderCare Online
Web site: http://www.ec-online.net

ElderWeb
Web site: http://www.elderweb.com

Empowering Caregivers
(Provides education, resources, emotional and spiritual support, forums, chats, newsletter, journal exercises, expert columns, and articles on care giving)
Phone: (212) 807-1204
Web site: http://www.care-givers.com

Enhanced Vision Systems
5882 Machine Drive
Huntington Beach, CA 92649
Phone: (888) 811-3161 or (714) 374-1829, Fax: (714) 374-1821
Web site: http://www.enhancedvision.com

Equal Employment Opportunity Commission
1801 L Street, NW
Washington, DC 20507
Phone: (800) 669-4000 or (202) 663-4900,
TDD: (202) 663-4494
Web site: http://www.eeoc.gov

Faith in Action National Network
Phone: (866) 839-8865
Web site: http://www.fianationalnetwork.org

Families USA Foundation
(Health care policies and resources)
1201 New York Avenue, NW
Washington, DC 20005
Phone: (202) 628-3030, Fax: (202) 347-2417
Web site: http://www.familiesusa.org

Family and Medical Leave Act (FMLA)
(Employee/Employer Advisor Web site)
Web site: http://www.dol.gov/elaws/fmla.htm

Family Caregiver Alliance
180 Montgomery Street, Suite 1100
San Francisco, CA 94104
Phone: (800) 445-8106 or (415) 434-3388
Web site: http://www.caregiver.org

FamilyDoctor.org
(Health information and advice for caregivers written and reviewed by physicians and patient educational professionals.)
American Academy of Family Physicians
11400 Tomahawk Creek Parkway
Leanwood, KS 66211
Phone: (800) 274-2237, Fax: (913) 906-6094
Web site: http://www.familydoctor.org/online/famdocen/home/seniors.html

Federal Government Web sites
White House: **http://www.whitehouse.gov**
House of Representatives: http://www.house.gov
Senate: http://www.senate.gov

Federal Trade Commission
(Regulates the funeral industry)
Consumer Response Center
600 Pennsylvania Avenue, NW
Washington, DC 20580
Phone: (877) 382-4357, TDD: (866) 653-4261
Web site: http://www.ftc.gov

Federation of State Medical Boards
(To find your state medical board)
P.O. Box 619850
Dallas, TX 75621
Phone: (817) 868-4000, Fax: (817) 868-4099
Web site: http://www.fsmb.org

Financial Industry Regulatory Authority (FINRA)
(Call for district office location)
Phone: (800) 289-9999 or (301) 590-6500
Web site: http://www.finra.org

Financial Planning Association
4100 E. Mississippi Avenue, Suite 400
Denver, CO 80246
Phone: (800) 322-4237 or (800) 945-4237
Web site: http://www.plannersearch.org

Find an Ombudsman Near You
(Each state has a central office that can refer you to an ombudsman in your area. You can reach your state's web site in just three clicks.)
National Citizens' Coalition for Nursing Home Reform
1828 L Street, NW, Suite 801
Washington, DC 20036
Phone: (202) 332-2275, Fax: (202) 332-2949
Web site: http://www.nccnhr.org

Fisher Center for Alzheimer's Research Foundation
(A comprehensive portal for caregivers, family members, people living with Alzheimer's, and anyone who has an interest in learning about and conquering this devastating disease)
One Intrepid Square
West 46th Street & 12th Avenue
New York, NY 10036
Phone: (800) 259-4636
Web site: http://www.alzinfo.org

Five Wishes
(Five Wishes is a document that helps people express how they want to be treated if they become seriously ill and unable to speak for themselves. It is unique among all other living will and health agent forms because it looks to all of a person's needs: medical, personal, emotional, and spiritual. Five Wishes also encourages discussing your wishes with your family and physician.)

Aging with Dignity
P.O. Box 1661
Tallahassee, FL 32302
820 E. Park Avenue, Suite D100
Tallahassee, FL 32301
Phone: (888) 594-7437 or (850) 681-2010
Web site: http://www.agingwithdignity.org/5wishes.html

FootExpress.com
(A great source of education and information on the treatment of foot, ankle and heel conditions)
Web site: http://www.footexpress.com

Funeral Consumers Alliance
33 Patchen Road
South Burlington, VT 05403
Phone: (800) 765-0107
Web site: http://www.funerals.org

Funeral Help Program (FHP)
(Advises consumers of their options and rights)
1236 Ginger Crescent
Virginia Beach, VA 23453
Phone: (877) 427-0220
Web site: http://www.funeral-help.com

Generations United
1331 H Street, NW, Suite 900
Washington, DC 20005
Phone: (202) 289-3979, Fax: (202) 289-3952
Web site: http://www.gu.org

Gerontological Society of America
1220 L Street, NW, Suite 901
Washington, DC 20005
Phone: (202) 842-1275, Fax: (202) 842-1150
Web site: http://www.geron.org

Government Directory
(The single best source of Government information)
Web site: http://www.govstartpage.com

Grands Place
154 Cottage Road
Enfield, CT 06082
Phone: (860) 763-5789
Web site: http://www.grandsplace.org

Gray Panthers
1612 K Street, NW
Washington, DC 20006
Phone: (800) 280-5362 or (202) 737-6637, Fax: (202) 737-1160
Web site: http://www.graypanthers.org

Grief Healing
Web site: http://www.griefhealing.com

Growth House
Phone: (415) 863-3045
Web site: http://www.growthhouse.org

Guide Dog Foundation for the Blind
371 East Jericho Turnpike
Smithtown, NY 11787
Phone: (800) 548-4337 or (631) 930-9000
Web site: http://www.guidedog.org

Guide to Choosing the Best Medicare Prescription Drug Plan
(Personalize your search for a Medicare Prescription Drug Plan that is right for you. This free site allows you to enter the prescription drugs you now take to find the most appropriate Medicare Prescription Drug Plan available in your area.)
Centers for Medicare and Medicaid Services
7500 Security Boulevard
Baltimore, MD 21244
Phone: (800) 633-4227
Web site: http://www.medicare.gov

Health A to Z
(In-depth health articles, online medical advice and health assessment tools such as nurse chat, symptom checker and the online health coach.)
50 Millstone Road, Building 200, Suite 160
East Windsor, NJ 08520
Phone: (609) 301-2169, Fax: (609) 426-4621
Web site: http://www.healthatoz.com

Health Insurance Association of America (HIAA)
(Offers insurance guides for consumers)
601 Pennsylvania Avenue, NW
South Building, Suite 500
Washington, DC 20004
Phone: (202) 778-3200, Fax: (202) 331-7487
Web site: http://www.hiaa.org

Healthfinder
(A gateway site to consumer health and human services information from the U.S. Department of Health and Human Services)
P.O. Box 1133
Washington, DC 20013
Web site: http://www.healthfinder.gov

Helping Hands Relocation
2973 Harbor Boulevard, #524
Costa Mesa, CA 92626
Phone: (800) 303-1877, Fax: (714) 435-0616
Web site: http://www.helpinghands-online.com

Hemlock Society
Phone: (800) 247-7421
Web site: http://www.hemlock.org

Hospice Association of America
228 Seventh Street, SE
Washington, DC 20003
Phone: (202) 546-4759, Fax: (202) 547-9559

Hospice Consumers Guide
(This easy to understand guide from the Hospice Association of America tells you what services hospice provides, how to get those services, how to pay for them, and what benefits you are entitled to under Medicare, Medicaid, and private insurance.)
Hospice Association of America
228 Seventh Street, SE
Washington, DC 20003
Phone: (202) 546-4759, Fax: (202) 547-9559
Web site: http://www.nahc.org/haa/consumerinfo.html

Hospice Foundation of America
Phone: (800) 854-3402
Web site: http://www.hospicefoundation.org

Insurance Information Institute
111 William Street
New York, NY 10038
Phone: (800) 331-1946, Fax: (212) 791-1807
Web site: http://www.iii.org

Insurance Institute for Highway Safety
1005 Glebe Road, Suite 800
Arlington, VA 22201
Phone: (703) 247-1500, Fax: (703) 247-1588
Web site: http://www.hwysafety.org

Internal Revenue Service
(Tax counseling for the elderly)
Phone: (800) 829-1040, TDD: (800) 829-4059
Web site: http://www.irs.gov

Joint Commission on Accreditation of Health Care Organizations (JCAHO)
One Renaissance Boulevard
Oakbrook Terrace, IL 60181
Phone: (630) 792-5000, Fax: (630) 792-5599
Web site: http://www.jcaho.org

Leadership Council of Aging Organizations
Phone: (202) 479-6970
Web site: http://www.lcao.org

Legal Services Corporation
(Legal help to low-income individuals in civil matters)
3333 K Street, NW, 3rd Floor
Washington, DC 20007
Phone: (202) 205-1500, Fax: (202) 337-6797
Web site: http://www.lsc.gov

Licensed Independent Network of CPA Financial Planners (LINC)
P.O. Box 1559
Columbia, TN 38402

Little Brothers — Friends of the Elderly
28 E. Jackson Boulevard, Suite 405
Chicago, IL 60604
Phone: (312) 829-3055, Fax: (312) 829-3077
Web site: http://www.little-brothers.org

Locate a Hospice Near You
(Locate a hospice near you. using one of the easiest hospice search utilities available. Search by state, county or zip code.)
Web site: http://www.hospicedirectory.org

Managing Work & Family, Inc.
912 Crain Street
Evanston, IL 60202
Phone: (847) 308-0919, Fax: (661) 885-7865
Web site: http://www.mwfam.com

Mayo Clinic
(Provides information on medical conditions, diet, exercise, and health)
Web site: http://www.mayohealth.org

Meals on Wheels Association of America
2035 S. Union Street
Alexandria, VA 22314
Phone: (703) 548-5558, Fax: (703) 548-8024
Web site: http://www.mowaa.org

MedicAlert
2323 Colorado Avenue
Turlock, CA 95382
Phone: (888) 633-4298, Fax: (209) 669-2450
Web site: http://www.medicalert.org

Medicare Hotline
Phone: (800) 633-4227, TDD: (877) 486-2048
Web site: http://www.medicare.gov

Medicare Nursing Home Comparison
(A wonderful research tool based on annual inspections of the nation's nursing homes. Provides detailed information about the past performance of every Medicare and Medicaid certified nursing home in the country.)
Centers for Medicare and Medicaid Services
7500 Security Boulevard
Baltimore, MD 21244
Phone: (800) 633-4227
Web site: http://www.medicare.gov

Medicare Rights Center Hotline
110 Maryland Avenue, NE, Suite 112
Washington, DC 20002
Phone: (202) 544-5561, Fax: (202) 544-5549
Web site: http://www.medicarerights.org

Medline
(Comprehensive online quality health care information assembled by the U.S. National Library of Medicine at the National Institutes of Health.)
U.S. National Library of Medicine
8600 Rockville Pike
Bethesda, MD 20894
Web site: http://www.nlm.nih.gov/medlineplus/

Multiple Sclerosis Association of America
706 Haddonfield Road
Cherry Hill, NJ 08002
Phone: (800) 532-7667 or (856) 488-4500, Fax: (856) 661-9797
Web site: http://www.msaa.com

National Academy of Elder Law Attorneys
1604 N. Country Club Road
Tucson, AZ 85716
Phone: (520) 881-4005, Fax: (520) 325-7925
Web site: http://www.naela.com

National Accessible Apartment Clearinghouse
4300 Wilson Boulevard, #400
Arlington, VA 22203
Phone: (800) 421-1221, Fax: (703) 248-9440
Web site: http://www.accessibleapartments.org

National Adult Day Services Association
85 S. Washington, Suite 316
Seattle, WA 98104
1-877-745-1440
Website: http://www.nadsa.org

National Amputation Foundation
40 Church Street
Malverne, NY 11565
Phone: (516) 887-3600, Fax: (516) 887-3667
Web site: http://www.nationalamputation.org

National Aphasia Association
350 Serenity Avenue, Suite 902
New York, NY 10001
Phone: (800) 922-4622
Web site: http://www.aphasia.org

National Asian/Pacific Resource Center on Aging (NAPCA)
Melbourne Tower
1511 Third Street, Suite 914
Seattle, WA 98101
Phone: (800) 336-2722 or (206) 624-1221, Fax: (206) 624-1023
Web site: http://www.napca.org

National Association for Continence (NAFC)
P.O. Box 1019
Charleston, SC 29402
Phone: (800) 252-3337 or (843) 377-0900, Fax: (843) 377-0905
Web site: http://www.nafc.org

National Association for Hispanic Elderly
(Provides information and referral services for elderly Hispanic people)
234 East Colorado Boulevard, Suite 300
Pasadena, CA 91101
Phone: (626) 564-1988

National Association for Home Care
228 Seventh Street, SE
Washington, DC 20003
Phone: (202) 547-7424, Fax: (202) 547-3540

National Association of Area Agencies on Aging
1730 Rhode Island Avenue, NW, Suite 1200
Washington, DC 20036
Phone: (202) 872-0888, Fax: (202) 872-0057
Web site: http://www.n4a.org

National Association of Insurance Commissioners
2301 McGee Street, Suite 800
Kansas City, MO 64108
Phone: (816) 842-3600, Fax: (816) 783-8175
Web site: http://www.naic.org

National Association of Personal Financial Advisors (NAPFA)
3250 N. Arlington Heights Road, Suite 109
Arlington Heights, IL 60004
Phone: (800) 366-2732 or (847) 483-5400, Fax: (847) 483-5415
Web site: http://www.napfa.org

National Association of Professional Geriatric Care Managers
1604 N. Country Club Road
Tucson, AZ 85716
Phone: (520) 881-8008, Fax: (520) 325-7925
Web site: http://www.caremanager.org

National Association of Senior Move Managers
(The only professional association in the country devoted to assisting older adults and families with the physical and emotional demands of downsizing, relocating, or modifying their homes)
P.O. Box 209
Hinsdale, IL 60522
Phone: (877) 606-2766; Fax: (630)230-3594
Web site: http://www.nasmm.org

National Association of Social Workers
750 First Street, NE, Suite 700
Washington, DC 20002
Phone: (202) 408-8600
Web site: http://www.socialworkers.org

National Association of the Deaf
8630 Fenton Street, Suite 820
Silver Spring, MD 20910
Phone: (301) 587-1788, Fax: (301) 587-1791, TDD: (301) 587-1789
Web site: http://www.nad.org

National Association of Unclaimed Property Administrators
(To search each state's database)
Web site: http://www.unclaimed.org

National Cancer Institute
(Federal government agency which funds and conducts research, clinical trials, and provides information for patients and their families)
NCI Public Inquiries Office
6116 Executive Boulevard, Suite 3036A
Bethesda, MD 20892
Phone: (800) 422-6237
Web site: http://www.cancer.gov

National Caregivers Library
901 Moorefield Park Drive, Suite 100
Richmond, VA 23236
Phone: (804) 327-1112
Web site: http://www.caregiverslibrary.org

National Caregiving Foundation
Phone: (800) 930-1357
Web site: http://www.caregivingfoundation.org

National Caucus and Center on Black Aged
1220 L Street, NW, Suite 800
Washington, DC 20005
Phone: (202) 637-8400, Fax: (202) 347-0895
Web site: http://www.ncba-aged.org

National Center for Home Equity Conversion (NCHEC)
(Consumer information on reverse mortgages)
360 Robert Street North, Suite 403
Saint Paul, MN 55101
Phone: (651) 222-6775, Fax: (651) 222-6797
Web site: http://www.reverse.org

National Center on Elder Abuse
c/o Center for Community Research & Services
University of Delaware
297 Graham Hall
Newark, DE 19716
Phone: (302) 831-3525, Fax: (302) 831-4225
Web site: http://www.ncea.aoa.gov

National Citizens' Coalition for Nursing Home Reform (NCCNHR)
1828 L Street, NW, Suite 801
Washington, DC 20036
Phone: (202) 332-2276, Fax: (202) 332-2949
Web site: http://www.nccnhr.org

National Committee for Quality Assurance (NCQA)
1100 13th Street, NW, Suite 1000
Washington, DC 20005
Phone: (888) 275-7585 or (202) 955-3500, Fax: (202) 955-3599
Web site: http://www.ncqa.org

National Committee to Preserve Social Security and Medicare
10 G Street, NE, Suite 600
Washington, DC 20002
Phone: (800) 966-1935, Fax: (202) 216-0451
Web site: http://www.ncpssm.org

National Consumers League
1701 K Street, NW, Suite 1200
Washington, DC 20006
Phone: (800) 876-7060 or (202) 835-3323, Fax: (202) 835-0747
Web site: http://www.nclnet.org

National Council of Senior Citizens
8403 Colesville Road, Suite 1200
Silver Spring, MD 20910
Phone: (888) 373-6467 or (301) 578-8800, Fax: (301) 578-8999

National Council on Aging
(A national network of more than 14,000 organizations that help older people remain healthy and independent, find jobs and increase access to benefits programs)
1901 L Street, NW, 4th Floor
Washington, DC 20036
Phone: (202) 479-1200, Fax: (202) 479-0735, TDD: (202) 479-6674
Web site: http://www.ncoa.org

National Family Caregivers Association (NFCA)
(Provides education, information, and support to improve the caregiver's quality of life)
10400 Connecticut Avenue, Suite 500
Kensington, MD 20895
Phone: (800) 896-3650 or (301) 942-6430, Fax: (301) 942-2302
Web site: http://www.nfcacares.org

National Fraud Information Center (NFIC)
c/o National Consumers League
1701 K Street, NW, Suite 1200
Washington, DC 20006
Phone: (800) 876-7060
Web site: http://www.fraud.org/welmes.htm

National Funeral Directors Association
400 C Street, NE
Washington, DC 20002
Phone: (202) 547-0441, Fax: (202) 547-0726
Web site: http://www.nfda.org

National Guardianship Association
174 Crestview Drive
Bellefonte, PA 16823
Phone: (877) 326-5992, Fax: (814) 355-2452
Web site: http://www.guardianship.org

National Headache Foundation
820 N. Orleans, Suite 217
Chicago, IL 60610
Phone: (888) 643-5552
Web site: http://www.headaches.org

National Health Information Center
P.O. Box 1133
Washington, DC 20013
Phone: (800) 336-4797, Fax: (301) 984-4256
Web site: http://www.health.gov/nhic

National Heart, Lung, and Blood Institute
(Provides information on diseases of the heart, lung, and blood)
P.O. Box 30105
Bethesda, MD 20824
Phone: (301) 592-8573, Fax: (240) 629-3246, TDD: (240) 629-3255
Web site: http://www.nhlbi.nih.gov

National Highway Traffic Safety Administration
1200 New Jersey Avenue, SE, West Building
Washington, DC 20590
Phone: (888) 327-4236, TDD: (800) 424-9153
Web site: http://www.nhtsa.dot.gov

National Indian Council on Aging
10501 Montgomery Boulevard, NE, Suite 210
Albuquerque, NM 87111
Phone: (508) 292-2001, Fax: (505) 292-1922
Web site: http://www.nicoa.org

National Institute of Arthritis and Musculoskeletal and Skin Diseases
1 AMS Circle
Bethesda, MD 20892
Phone: (301) 495-4267, Fax: (301) 718-6366
Web site: http://www.niams.nih.gov

National Institute of Diabetes, Digestive, and Kidney Diseases
(Provides information on these diseases)
NIDDK — NIH
Building 31, Room 9A06
31 Center Drive, MSC 2560
Bethesda, MD 20892
Phone: (301) 496-3583
Web site: http://www.niddk.nih.gov

National Institute of Mental Health
(Provides information on symptoms, diagnosis, and treatment of mental illness)
6001 Executive Boulevard, Room 8184, MSC 9663
Bethesda, MD 20892
Phone: (866) 615-6464 or (301) 443-4513, Fax: (301) 443-4279, TDD: (866) 415-8051
Web site: http://www.nimh.nih.gov

National Institute of Neurological Disorders and Stroke
(Describes brain attacks and offers prevention strategies)
P.O. Box 5801
Bethesda, MD 20824
Phone: (800) 352-9424 or (301) 496-5751, TDD: (301) 468-5981
Web site: http://www.ninds.nih.gov

National Institute on Aging (NIA)
Public Information Office, Building 31, Room 5C27
31 Center Drive, MSC 2292
Bethesda, MD 20892
Phone: (800) 222-2225 or (301) 496-1752,
Web site: http://www.nih.gov/nia

National Institute on Deafness and Other Communication Disorders
31 Center Drive, MSC 2320
Bethesda, MD 20892
Phone: (800) 241-1044 or (301) 496-7243, TDD: (800) 241-1055
Web site: http://www.nidcd.nih.gov

National Institutes of Health (NIH)
(Offers consumer health information, fact sheets, brochures, articles, and handbooks)
9000 Rockville Pike
Bethesda, MD 20892
Phone: (301) 496-4000, TDD: (301) 402-9612
Web site: http://www.nih.gov

National Insurance Consumer Helpline
Phone: (800) 942-4242

National Library Service for the Blind and Physically Handicapped Hotline
(A free library program of Braille and audio materials by postage-free mail – through the Library of Congress)
Phone: (800) 424-9100
Web site: http://www.loc.gov/nls

National Long Term Care Ombudsman Resource Center
(Provides support, technical assistance, and training to the 53 State Long Term Care Ombudsman Programs. Check out the Ombudsman Desk Reference for sections on long term care statistics, federal, state and local agency contacts, resources and general references.)
1828 L Street, NW, Suite 801
Washington, DC 20036
Phone: (202) 332-2275, Fax: (202) 332-2949
Web site: http://www.ltcombudsman.org

National Mental Health Association
2000 N. Beauregard Street, Sixth Floor
Alexandria, VA 22311
Phone: (800) 969-6642 or (703) 684-7722
Web site: http://www.nmha.org

National Network of Estate Planning Attorneys
3500 De Pauw Boulevard, Suite 2090
Indianapolis, IN 46268
Phone: (800) 638-8681
Web site: http://www.netplanning.com

National Osteoporosis Foundation
(Provides advocacy, information, and support for patients)
1232 22nd Street, NW
Washington, DC 20037
Phone: (800) 231-4222 or (202) 223-2226
Web site: http://www.nof.org

National Registry of Rehabilitation Technology Suppliers
Phone: (800) 976-7787 or (303) 948-1080, Fax: (303) 948-1528
Web site: http://www.nrrts.org

National Rehabilitation Information Center (NARIC)
8201 Corporate Drive, Suite 600
Landover, MD 20785
Phone: (800) 346-2742
Web site: http://www.naric.com

National Resource and Policy Center on Housing and Long Term Care
(Information about shared housing)
c/o Administration on Aging
One Massachusetts Avenue, Suites 4100/5100
Washington, DC 20201
Phone: (202) 619-0724, Fax: (202) 357-3555

National Respite Locator Service
Web site: http://chtop.org/arch/national-respite-locator.html

National Reverse Mortgage Lenders Association
(The national association dedicated to understanding and use of reverse mortgages)
Web site: http://www.reversemortgage.org

National Safety Council
1121 Spring Lake Drive
Itasca, IL 60143
Phone: (800) 621-7619 or (630) 285-1121, Fax: (630) 285-1315
Web site: http://www.nsc.org

National Senior Citizen Law Center
1444 Eye Street, NW, Suite 1100
Washington, DC 20005
Phone: (202) 289-6976, Fax: (202) 289-7224
Web site: http://www.nsclc.org

National Sleep Foundation
(Provides information on sleep disorders and treatment)
1522 K Street, NW, Suite 500
Washington, DC 20005
Phone: (202) 347-3471, Fax: (202) 347-3472
Web site: http://www.sleepfoundation.org

National Stroke Association
(Offers a wide range of information on strokes)
9707 E. Easter Lane
Centennial, CO 80112
Phone: (800) 787-6537
Web site: http://www.stroke.org

National Vaccine Information Center
204 Mill Street, Suite B1
Vienna, VA 22180
Phone: (703) 938-0342, Fax: (703) 938-5768
Web site: http://www.909shot.com

National Women's Health Information Center
Office of Women's Health, DHHS
(Focuses on women's health issues)
200 Independence Avenue, SW, Room 712E
Washington, DC 20201
Phone: (800) 994-9662 or (202) 690-7560, Fax: (202) 205-2631, TDD: (888) 220-5446
Web site: http://www.4women.gov

North American Securities Administrators Association (NASAA)
750 First Street, NE, Suite 1140
Washington, DC 20002
Phone: (888) 846-2722 or (202) 737-0900, Fax: (202) 783-3571
Web site: http://www.nasaa.org

Nursing Home Abuse Resource
(Nursing Home abuse portal offering general information about abuse with links to nursing home abuse law firms)
Web site: http://www.nursing-home-abuse-resource.com

Older Women's League (OWL)
3300 N. Fairfax Drive, Suite 218
Arlington, VA 22201
Phone: (703) 812-7990, Fax: (703) 812-0687
Web site: http://www.owl-national.org

Paralyzed Veterans of America
(Focuses on special needs of veterans with spinal cord dysfunction)
National Headquarters
801 18th Street, NW
Washington, DC 20006
Phone: (800) 424-8200, TDD: (800) 795-4327
Web site: http://www.pva.org

Parkinson's Disease Resource Locator
(National Parkinson's site. Use it to locate affiliated chapters, outreach centers, physicians and local support groups.)
Parkinson's Action Network
1025 Vermont Avenue, NW, Suite 1120
Washington, DC 20005
Phone: (800) 850-4726, Fax: (202) 638-7257
Web site: http://www.parkinsonsaction.org

Parkinson's Resource Organization
(Provides information, education, and support for people affected by Parkinson's)
74090 El Paseo, Suite 102
Palm Desert, CA 92260
Phone: (877) 775-4111 or (760) 773-5628, Fax: (760) 773-9803
Web site: http://www.parkinsonsresource.org

Partnership for Caring
(Advocates to ensure comfort and care for every dying person)
1620 Eye Street, NW, Suite 202
Washington, DC 20006
Phone: (800) 658-8898
Web site: http://www.partnershipforcaring.org

Podiatry Network
(Source of foot care information)
3663 NASA Parkway, Suite 606
Seabrook, TX 77586
Web site: http://www.podiatrynetwork.com

Prevent Medication Errors
(A report to the President of the United States in 2000 by the Agency for Healthcare Research. Lists twenty steps you can take to prevent errors in medication and treatment.)
Center for Quality Improvement and Patient Safety (CQuIPS)
540 Gaither Road
Rockville, MD 20850
Phone: (301) 427-1364
Web site: http://www.quic.gov/report/index.htm

Pro Se Law Center
c/o Maryland Legal Assistance Network
15 Charles Plaza, Suite 101
Baltimore, MD 21201
Phone: (410) 576-9494
Web site: http://www.pro-selaw.org

Schizophrenia.com
Web site: http://www.schizophrenia.com

Schizophrenics Anonymous
c/o National Schizophrenia Foundation
403 Seymour Avenue, Suite 202
Lansing, MI 48933
Phone: (800) 482-9534 or (517) 485-7168, Fax: (517) 485-7180

Securities and Exchange Commission (SEC)
Office of Investor Education and Assistance
450 Fifth Street, NW
Washington, DC 20549
Phone: (800) 732-0330 or (202) 942-7040, Fax: (202) 942-9634
Web site: http://www.sec.gov

Self Help for Hard of Hearing People
(Provides links and information on hearing loss and hearing aids)
7910 Woodmont Avenue, Suite 1200
Bethesda, MD 20814
Phone: (301) 657-2248, Fax: (301) 913-9413
Web site: http://www.hearingloss.org

Senior Law Web site
(Information about elder law and related subjects)
Web site: http://www.seniorlaw.com

Senior Resource
(Web site offers retirees extensive information on finance, housing, insurance and health)
4521 Campus Drive, #131
Irvine, CA 92612
Web site: http://www.seniorresource.com

Silvercare Productions
(Joy Loverde Employee Eldercare Workshops)
1560 N. Sandburg Terrace, Suite 2509
Chicago, IL 60610
Phone: (312) 642-3611, Fax: (312) 642-8110
Web site: http://www.elderindustry.com

Silvert's Clothing
(Provides men's and women's clothing designed for Alzheimer's, arthritis, foot problems, incontinence, scoliosis and those who are wheelchair bound.)
3280 Steeles Avenue West, Suite 18
Concord (Toronto), Ontario L4K 2Y2
Phone: (800) 387-7088, Fax: (905) 738-6236
Web site: http://www.Eldercare1.com/sil

Social Security Administration
Windsor Park Building
6401 Security Boulevard
Baltimore, MD 21235
Phone: (800) 772-1213, TDD: (800) 325-0778
Web site: http://www.ssa.gov

Society of Financial Service Professionals
17 Campus Boulevard, Suite 201
Newtown Square, PA 19073
Phone: (888) 243-2258 or (610) 526-2500, Fax: (610) 527-1499
Web site: http://www.financialpro.org

Stroke Family
(Provides stroke and speech recovery kits that speed recovery in the home)
Phone: (877) 835-3157
Web site: http://www.strokefamily.org

The Lighthouse National Center for Vision and Aging
(Provides helpful information for those with vision problems)
111 East 59th Street
New York, NY 10022
Phone: (800) 829-0500 or (212) 821-9200, Fax: (212) 821-9707, TDD: (212) 821-9713
Web site: http://www.lighthouse.org

United States Consumer Product Safety Commission
4330 East West Highway
Bethesda, MD 20814
Phone: (800) 638-2772 or (301) 504-7923, Fax: (301) 504-0124
Web site: http://www.cpsc.gov

United States Department of Housing and Urban Development (HUD)
(Provides low-cost housing)
451 7th Street, SW
Washington, DC 20410
Phone: (202) 708-1112
Web site: http://www.hud.gov

USA.gov for Seniors
(Provides information on health care, benefits, long-term care, caregivers, and more)
Web site: http://www.seniors.gov

Visiting Nurse Associations of America
900 19th Street, NW, Suite 200
Washington, DC 20006
Phone: (202) 384-1420, Fax: (202) 384-1444
Web site: http://www.vnaa.org

Volunteers of America
1660 Duke Street
Alexandria, VA 22314
Phone: (800) 899-0089, Fax: (703) 341-7000
Web site: http://www.voa.org

Well Spouse Association
(Help for those who are caring for spouses)
30 East 40th Street, PH
New York, NY 10018
Phone: (800) 838-0879 or (212) 685-8815, Fax: (212) 685-8676
Web site: http://www.wellspouse.org

Work & Family Connection, Inc.
(Clearinghouse for work/life issues and practices)
5197 Beachside Drive
Minnetonka, MN 55343
Phone: (800) 487-7898 or (952) 936-7898, Fax: (952) 935-0122
Web site: http://www.workfamily.com

Write Your Senator or Representative
Address envelope to:
Senator (Name), United States Senate
Washington, DC 20510
Representative (Name), United States House of Representatives
Washington, DC 20515

About the Author ... Martin R. Sabel

Martin Sabel is an expert on the financial issues of aging.

Known as "Mr. Eldercare," Martin provides his practical knowledge with a gentle touch to guide family caregivers safely over the bumpy roads of caring for elderly parents. His warm style of straight talk relieves the fear, anxiety and worry families face.

His dad's illnesses in 1994 opened up Martin's eyes to a fragmented, unfriendly and exasperating elder care delivery system. That year he established Houston's first financial planning organization dedicated to helping families manage the burden of late-life health care.

As a practicing financial gerontologist and paralegal he understands the frustrations, worries and fears family caregivers deal with on a daily basis. His long time involvement with families led him to conclude that the emotional costs of care can equal or exceed the financial costs.

To provide additional caregiver support and education, Martin created his weekly "Ask Mr. Eldercare" Internet call-in radio show that provides instant, interactive access to elder care experts. Find out more about the show by visiting http://www.SurvivingEldercare.com/BTR.

Martin works with family members and organizations that want to help family caregivers lessen the financial and emotional burdens of caring for elderly parents. As a professional speaker and author, he brings a message of hope and empowerment to families across America facing critical elder care decisions.

He encourages readers to contact him directly with concerns and questions. He may be reached through his radio show or his website: http://www.SurvivingEldercare.com.

Since 2001, Martin has been the expert on the financial issues of aging and senior paralegal for the Houston Elder Law Firm of Mulder and Freedman. He lives in Houston with his wife of 27 years, a son and a self-centered cat named "Dude."